The Courtauld Gallery
at Somerset House

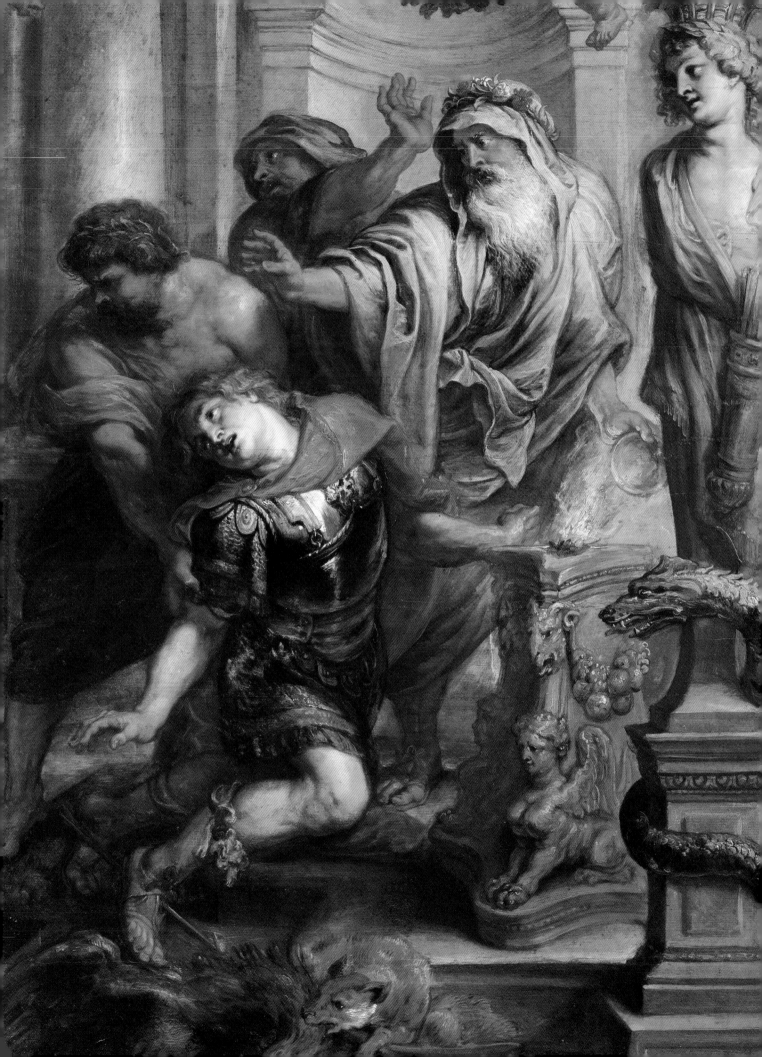

The Courtauld Gallery
at Somerset House

Introduction by JOHN MURDOCH

COURTAULD INSTITUTE OF ART

in association with

THAMES & HUDSON

ACKNOWLEDGMENTS

Paintings by Pierre Bonnard, Paul Signac and Jean-Edouard Vuillard © ADAGP, Paris, and DACS, London, 1998; painting by Oskar Kokoschka © DACS 1998; painting by Ben Nicholson © Angela Verren-Taunt 1998. All rights reserved DACS.

With the exception of the items listed below, all illustrations are from the Courtauld Gallery collections: p. 6 Courtesy, Courtaulds plc; p. 8 Copyright *Country Life*; p. 21 By permission of the President and Council of the Royal Society; p. 23 Copyright British Museum.

On the cover:
(front) Vincent van Gogh, *The Crau at Arles: Peach Trees in Flower*, 1889 (detail); (back) Frederick Mackenzie (c.1787–1854), *Porchway, Somerset House*, pencil and watercolour. Both Courtauld Gallery
Frontispiece:
Rubens, *The Death of Achilles*, c.1630–5 (detail)

For the Courtauld Institute of Art
Editorial supervision and co-ordination by
Elizabeth Foy and Christine Butterfield

First published in 1998 by the Courtauld Institute of Art, University of London, in association with Thames & Hudson Ltd, London
Reprinted 2002

First published in paperback in the United States of America in 1999 by Thames & Hudson Inc., 500 Fifth Avenue, New York, New York 10110

A catalogue record for this book is available from the British Library
Library of Congress Catalog Card Number 98-61031

ISBN   0-500-95993-5 (Courtauld Institute edition)
        0-500-28091-6 (Thames & Hudson edition)

Colour reproductions by Eurocrom 4 srl, Villorba, Treviso, Italy

Printed and bound in Singapore by C S Graphics

CONTENTS

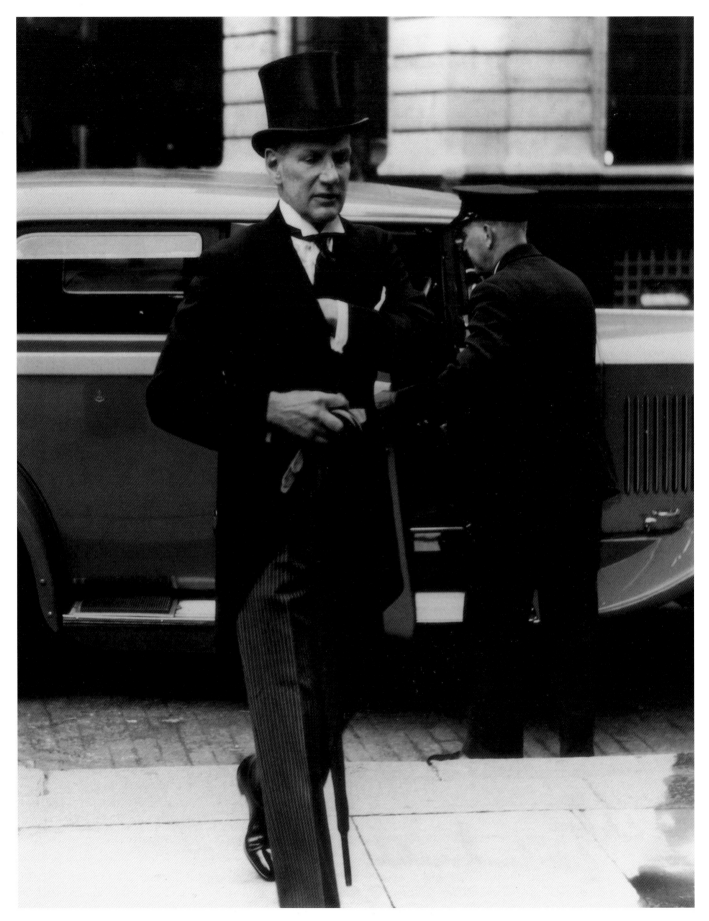

Samuel Courtauld, July 1936.

INTRODUCTION
by John Murdoch

The Courtauld Gallery contains some 530 paintings, over 26,000 drawings and prints, and significant collections of medieval, Renaissance and modern sculpture, ceramics, metalwork, furniture and textiles. Since 1990 it has occupied the central part of the North Block of Somerset House, one of the most important eighteenth-century buildings in Europe, where it was reunited with its parent body, the Courtauld Institute of Art, one of the world's leading organizations for research into and teaching of the history of Western art. The Gallery is open to the public and, like any other major art museum, provides a full range of public services. Its special character, however, derives from two aspects of its history: first, that it directly supports the teaching programmes of the Courtauld Institute and the University of London; and second, that it is made up of a series of formerly private collections, each of considerable significance in the history of collecting, and each containing works of art of memorable beauty and historical importance. Unlike most of the other major art museums in London, however, it is wholly a creation of the twentieth century. It owes its inception to the imagination and generosity of Samuel Courtauld, who established it, originally in his house, 20 Portman Square, as a memorial to his wife Elizabeth following her death in 1931.

Samuel Courtauld (1876–1947)

Courtauld was descended from a Huguenot family which first settled in London and the south-east of England in the late seventeenth century; they were active as silversmiths in the eighteenth century, and became prosperous as manufacturers of silk crepe for mourning throughout the nineteenth. With the decline in demand for mourning clothes at the turn of the century, the family firm established itself as the leading world producer of the first important artificial textile, known as Rayon, and, expanding to meet the huge demand created by World War I, became the great multi-national company still in existence today. Samuel Courtauld became its Chairman in 1921, inheriting both the accumulated cash reserves of the company built up during the war years, and the glittering prospects for expansion provided by the new peacetime industries, from clothing to motor-vehicle tyres. In the course of the necessary financial restructuring of the company, he became, as a major shareholder, immensely rich, but as a man of high spiritual and moral consciousness, he shared also the common post-war determination to make the world a better and more 'modern'

place. He and his wife therefore engaged actively in London charities, and were invariably among the earliest and most generous donors to worthy causes, especially those directed at the aesthetic and spiritual advancement of mankind. Elizabeth was principally associated with the establishment and financing of the Covent Garden Opera and with the Wigmore Hall concerts founded by Malcolm Sargent in 1929, and Samuel with the National and Tate Galleries, the building of his own collection, and the encouragement of young British artists.

Courtauld's interest in art had originally been aroused when he saw Italian Renaissance painting in which, during his wedding journey to Florence with Elizabeth in 1901, he 'perceived a wonderful mastery allied with strong emotion and with life itself; . . . strong and exciting currents still flowing beneath the surface of the paint'. Such responses were definitively reawakened by the spectacle of the Hugh Lane collection, shown at the Tate Gallery in 1917. It demonstrated to him that the formal and emotional qualities of the Old Master tradition were alive and well in the 'modern' French school, especially in Manet, Renoir and Degas. It was this perception which led, as part of his charitable enterprises, to his determination to secure a suitable representation of works by these painters in the British national collections. He therefore gave £50,000 to the nation, to be spent on paintings which would be chosen, largely by himself, with the agreement of the respective Directors of the Tate and National Galleries. The purchases which he made now count among the most famous nineteenth-century works in the National Gallery – Renoir's *Première Sortie,* Degas's *Young Spartans,* Manet's *Servante des Bocks,* Van Gogh's *Sunflowers,* Seurat's *Bathing Party,* and many others. At the same time, he began acquiring works for his own private collection, acting – as he did with his public purchases – partly on the advice of the dealer Percy Moore Turner, but principally in accordance with his own sense of the formal and emotional properties of particular works. In the private collection, as it can largely now be seen in the Courtauld Gallery, there is evidence of some system, both of emotional or visual balance between individual works, and of an effort to represent in depth a period or type of painting, such as the early paintings by Renoir, or Cézanne as a painter of landscape. By 1925, Courtauld knew that the paintings were to hang in the house that he and his wife acquired at this time, the great aristocratic town-house of the Dowager Countess of Home, built by Robert Adam in 1774. Under their supervision, the house was painstakingly restored, the pictures hung by Percy Moore Turner, and the Courtaulds, with their only child, a

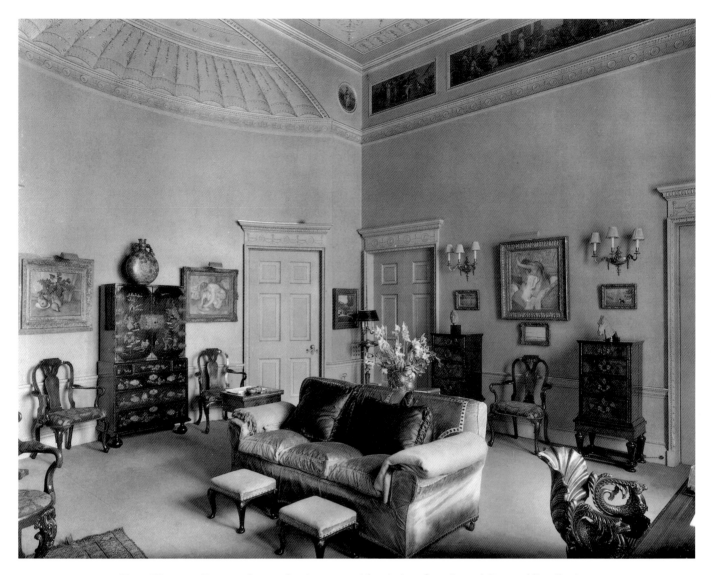

Home House, 20 Portman Square: drawing room with paintings from Samuel Courtauld's collection.

daughter named Sydney after her paternal grandfather, moved in, intending the house to be a centre and symbol of a modernity in touch with all that was best in the past. Their entertaining was spectacular. At one party Courtauld took Sydney and her new husband, R.A. Butler, aside and said, 'I hope you will both understand if I give this house and its contents to the nation.' Three years later, in 1929, while on holiday in Canada, Mrs Courtauld suffered the first painful symptoms of cancer. In the same year, the collapse of stock prices on Wall Street and the first signs of anti-monopolistic trade legislation in the U.S. Congress signalled that for companies like Courtaulds the halcyon days were over. Samuel Courtauld stopped collecting; his wife died on Christmas Day 1931, and in her memory he established the house, their joint enterprise, which he could no longer bear to live in, to be a centre for the international community of artists, art historians, museum curators and critics, who would be enrolled in an organization known as the Home House Society. With supporting trusts for the maintenance of the house and its

collections, the Home House Society (today known as the Samuel Courtauld Trust) assumed ownership of a major part of Samuel Courtauld's private collection in 1932 and 1934, acquiring the rest, except for a number of pictures which were bequeathed by Courtauld to members of his family and particular friends, following his death in 1947.

Arthur Lee, Viscount Lee of Fareham (1868–1947)

It was Arthur Lee who conceived the idea that Britain should possess an institution for the teaching of art history to the rising generations of museum curators, critics and scholars. A soldier, diplomat, politician and administrator of great distinction, he had served extensively in Canada and the United States, marrying the daughter of a New York banker, and becoming an admirer of East Coast 'brahmin' culture, especially as exemplified at Harvard University and the newly founded Fogg Art

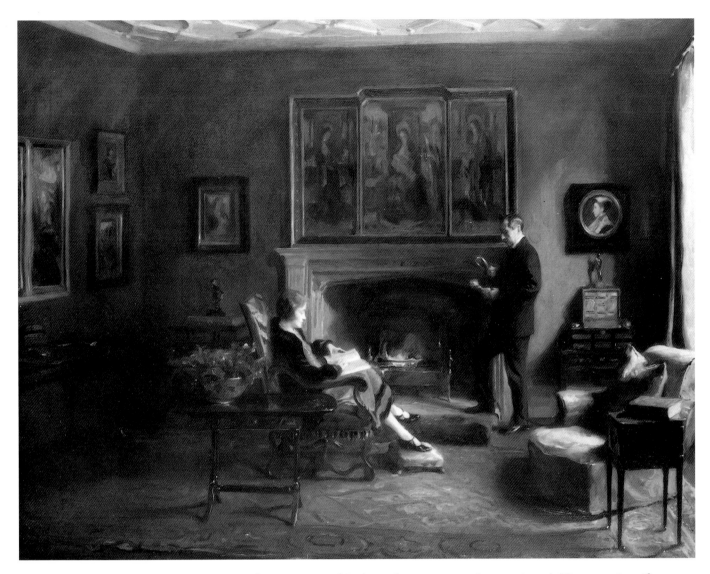

Philip de Laszlo, *Interior: The Viscount and Viscountess Lee of Fareham*, oil on canvas, 1925 (81.9 x 106.7 cm). Viscountess Lee gift.

Museum. Having formed a large collection of furniture and works of art at Chequers, his house in Buckinghamshire, in 1917 he and his wife Ruth turned it into a Trust to be used as an official country residence for successive Prime Ministers. He forthwith began a second collection, which he intended eventually to support the teaching of the history of art in a suitable university institution. In 1927 these ideas began to reach fruition when he persuaded Sir Gregory Foster, Vice-Chancellor of the University of London, to take the necessary steps. By 1929, the proposal had been approved by the Council, a suitable site earmarked on University land in Bloomsbury, curricula outlined and a possible director identified. Lee himself undertook to raise the necessary money, securing major contributions from Lord Duveen, Sir Robert Witt, Sir Herbert Cook, Alderman John Gross of Sheffield, Sir Martin Conway, and from Samuel Courtauld. But in the deteriorating economic circumstances, funds remained short of the amount required, and throughout the next two years little happened. Even Courtauld, whom Lee

approached for further help, was feeling the pinch, so instead of giving more money he suggested that the new institution, with its new director W.G. Constable, should move into the empty house at 20 Portman Square as a temporary measure, until the economy improved and the site in Bloomsbury could be developed. The Institute accordingly opened, accepting its first cohort of students in the autumn of 1932. In the event, the long Depression of the 1930s followed by World War II meant that the Institute never did effect the move to Bloomsbury, beside the Warburg Library, which Arthur Lee also personally intervened to save and bring to England from Hamburg in 1934, as part of the new institution. Lee declined the honour of having the Institute named after him, suggesting instead that, in recognition of the crucial role played by Courtauld in bringing the project to fruition, it should be named The Courtauld Institute of Art.

Under that name, and in the great house in Portman Square, the Institute acquired much of its special, intimate and, some would say, *élite* character. Courtauld himself seems to have been

9

pleased with its development, which gave a practical point to his establishment of the Home House Society. Lee died in 1947, bequeathing his collection to the University of London for the use of the Courtauld Institute, but with a life interest to his wife. In 1955 it was formally decided that the Institute would remain in Portman Square, and that the works of art should instead be displayed in purpose-built galleries on the site beside the Warburg Institute in Bloomsbury. For the opening of the galleries in 1958, Ruth Lee resigned her interest in the collection, which thus constituted the principal part of the historic displays in the new galleries.

The Lee Collection, it must be remembered, was always intended to provide exemplars for teaching. Beauty, fame and brilliant condition were less important to Lee than the relationship of a particular painting to the historical development of art as a whole. As a trustee of both the National Gallery and the Wallace Collection, he was well aware that the greatest works of art would be available in the national institutions in London, but that 'background', both in stylistic and technical terms, was

nonetheless necessary for academic study. Thus, the close craft relationship between painters, gilders, carvers and joiners in the Italian Renaissance workshops can be studied in Lee's group of painted marriage chests, which include the spectacular and extremely important Morelli-Nerli *cassoni* of 1472. Lee's relatively academic criteria did not indeed impede him from acquiring world-famous masterpieces, such as Rubens's sketch for the Antwerp *Descent from the Cross*, Cranach's *Adam and Eve*, or even, among his English pictures, Eworth's *Sir John Luttrell*, and the Lely *Concert Party* (all reproduced in this book).

The other founding collections

The names of Martin Conway (1856–1937) and Robert Witt (1872–1952) have remained familiar to generations of art historians through their collections of photographs documenting architecture, sculpture and the applied arts, and European painting. These constitute respectively the Conway and the Witt

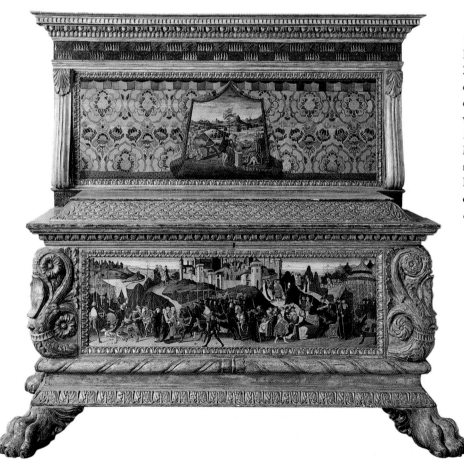

Cassone (chest for household linen), Florence, 1472; one of a pair carved by Zanobi di Domenico and with painted decoration by Jacopo del Sellaio and Biagio d'Antonio. The two chests, each 212 cm in width and featuring scenes from Livy's *Histories*, were commissioned by Lorenzo di Matteo di Morelli on the occasion of his marriage to Vaggia di Tanai di Francesco Nerli; the arms of the two families are displayed on the front corners of each *cassone*. Lee Collection.

Opposite, above:
Muirhead Bone (1876–1954),
Sir Robert Witt in his Library.
Witt Collection.

Opposite below:
Thomas Gainsborough (1727–88),
Wooded Landscape with Herdsmen Driving Cattle over a Bridge.
Witt Collection.

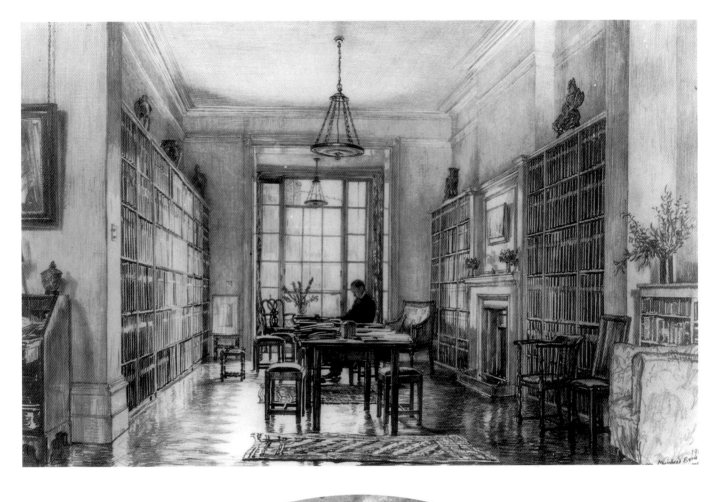

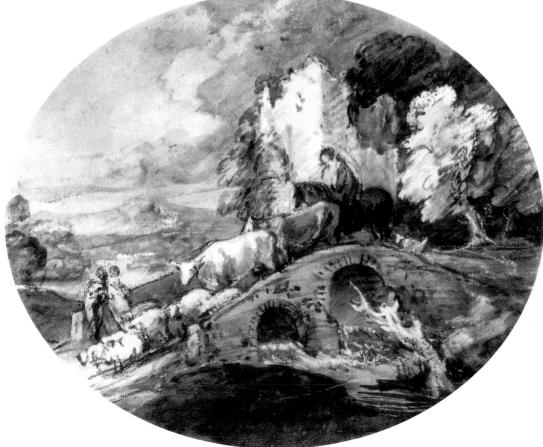

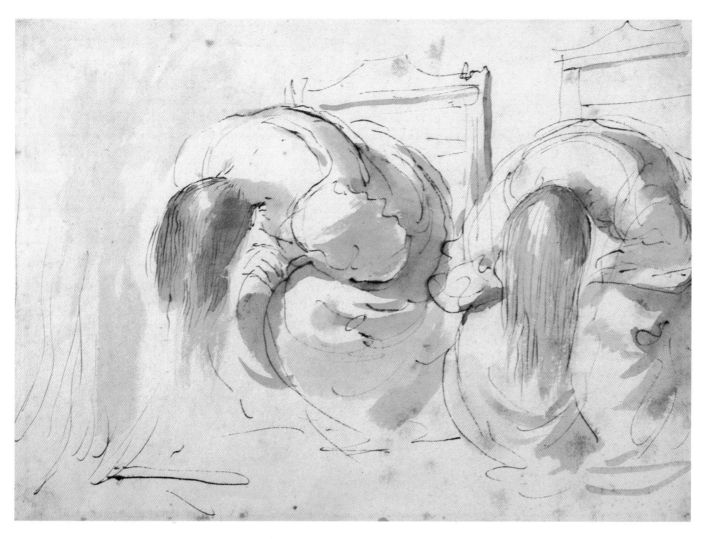

Guercino (Gianfrancesco Barbieri; 1591–1666), *Women Drying their Hair*. Witt Collection.

Left: Roger Fry, *Self-portrait*, oil on canvas, 1928.

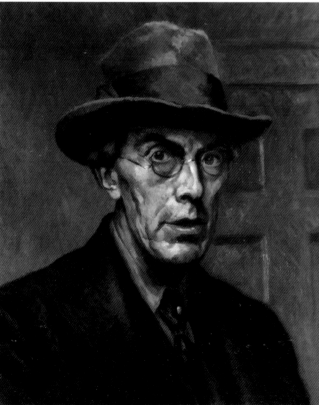

libraries of the Courtauld Institute, and are a vital resource for research by the whole community of scholars and art dealers in Britain. As well as photographs of paintings, Witt collected prints, firstly reproductive prints, but subsequently original Old Master prints and drawings for their own sake. As with Lee, his approach to works of art on paper was primarily academic, seeking to ensure the representation, for example, of the lesser Netherlandish masters, rather than concentrating on the great names which were, of course, already available for study at the British Museum. Again, however, the collection contains individual sheets which have become famous, such as the Bruegel *Kermesse at Hoboken* of 1559, and whole groups, such as the stunning series of drawings by Guercino, which certainly rival in quality those in the British Museum and Royal Collections. Witt also followed Lee's example in bequeathing his collections to the University, and for long they remained part of the Witt Library, becoming fully integrated with the principal collections in the Gallery, and open to the public in a purpose-built Print Room, only in 1990.

Among the public supporters of Lee's initiative in founding the Courtauld Institute was Roger Fry (1866–1934), formerly Curator of Old Master paintings at the Metropolitan Museum, New York, and subsequently a key promoter of 'modern' art in Britain, who imparted through his critical writings an enthusiasm for, and belief in the spiritual significance of art, which became a substitute for religion in many readers, such as Samuel Courtauld. It was possibly with Courtauld, therefore, rather than with Lee, that he felt the greater sympathy, recognizing in the former a readiness to support the living arts, and to find aesthetic excellence outside the canon of academic art history. Fry bequeathed to Courtauld's Home House Society examples of his own paintings, important designs by the artists associated with the Omega Workshops (founded by him in 1913), and objects, such as the African *Head*, which, within the Fry aesthetic, were accorded at least equal status with the greatest works of European art. Fry's intention was that his collection should be seen in a special room in Home House, in association with Courtauld's pictures, there constituting a firm declaration in favour of an 'open' modernism in art.

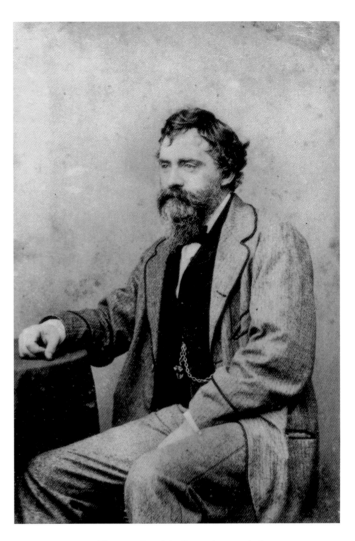

Thomas Gambier Parry (1816–88).

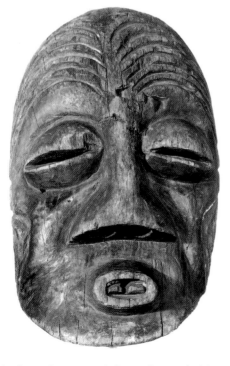

Head, African dancing mask from Ulvira, Lake Tanganyika; height 61 cm. Fry Collection.

The later Benefactors

Established in Woburn Square and connected to the outside world by a small and famously slow lift, the combined collections after 1958 began to acquire their reputation as 'London's best-kept secret': amazing in quality, and a wonderfully private experience for the few visitors, including the students of the Courtauld Institute, who found their way there. The success of the Gallery soon led to other benefactions, the first of which was the bequest in 1966 by Mark Gambier-Parry of the greater part of the collection formed by his grandfather, Thomas Gambier Parry (1816–88) for his house, Highnam Court, in Gloucestershire. Like Thomas Roscoe and Walter Bromley Davenport, Thomas Gambier Parry was one of a small group of nineteenth-century British collectors who appreciated the aesthetic and historical importance of the Italian 'primitives'. His collection is thus principally famous for the gold-ground paintings of the fourteenth and fifteenth centuries, such as the Crucifixion polyptych by Bernardo Daddi and *The Coronation of the Virgin*

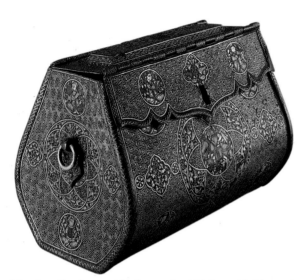

Islamic wallet, brass with silver and gold inlay, mid-thirteenth century. Gambier-Parry Collection.

by Lorenzo Monaco. Beyond the paintings, however, the collection extends into fields which, in the mid-nineteenth century, were also beginning to attract scholarly attention, such as French ivory carving, Limoges enamels, Italian maiolica and even Islamic silver-inlay metalwork. The collection was published in a special edition of the *Burlington Magazine* in March 1967, with articles by the leading Anglo-American scholars in the various fields.

The announcement of the Gambier-Parry Bequest was quickly followed by the bequest to the University in 1967 of the collection of English watercolours formed by Dr William Wycliffe Spooner (1882–1967) and his wife Mercie. In combination with the English eighteenth-century drawings in the Witt Collection, the Spooner Collection (among post-war collections second only to that formed by Paul Mellon in the 1950s and early 1960s) helped to establish the Gallery as one of the major centres for the study of English draughtsmanship. Mostly in superb condition, the watercolours include notable works by J.R. Cozens and Francis Towne, and were immediately made the subject of a special exhibition. A few years later, with the death of Sir Stephen Courtauld (1883–1974), the younger brother of Samuel, the potential strength of the English displays was increased with the bequest of a group of drawings by J.M.W. Turner, both major finished pieces such as the *Crook of Lune* from the Richmondshire series, and examples of the artist's astonishing, essentially private sketches, such as the *Storm over Margate Sands*. Like all works of art on paper, these watercolours can be displayed only occasionally, but they also soon formed

the subject of a special exhibition in 1974, and are now always available to be seen by appointment in the Gallery Print Room.

The 1970s closed with one of the greatest single benefactions ever received by a British gallery. This was the collection built up by Count Antoine Seilern (1901–78), born in England, the son of Count Carl Seilern and his wife, the American-born newspaper heiress Antoinette Woerischoffer (1875–1901), who died at his birth. With characteristic modesty, he originally intended that his bequest to the Home House Society should bear his mother's name rather than his own, but settled instead for the 'Princes Gate Collection', after the location of his London house.

Having been in his youth a keen hunter of big game, and a race-horse breeder and owner, he developed a serious academic interest in the history of art, and became a close friend of Johannes Wilde, at that time a curator at the Kunsthistorisches Museum, Vienna, and subsequently Deputy Director of the Courtauld Institute. Wilde, one of the most acute connoisseurs in Europe of the technical qualities of works of art, together with the great Dutch scholar Ludwig Burchard and the Austrian restorer Sebastian Isepp, advised Seilern on his acquisitions and on the series of catalogues raisonnés which Seilern progressively printed throughout his life for private circulation. Many of his most significant acquisitions were made through James Byam Shaw of Colnaghi's, and they reflect not only Seilern's essentially scholarly approach to collecting – as in the systematic groupings of sketches by Rubens and Tiepolo – but also a brilliant opportunism in securing great finished works of art from all schools and periods. These range from the *Entombment* triptych by the Master of Flémalle, through the great Rubens *Landscape by Moonlight*, and include world-famous drawings by all the principal European draughtsmen, such as Michelangelo's *Dream of Human Life*. Though the centre of his intellectual life was undoubtedly in the great tradition of European Old Master painting and drawing, Seilern, like Courtauld, was also deeply interested in art as a living process. It is to Seilern accordingly that the Gallery owes the presence of one of its most important twentieth-century works, the enormous *Prometheus* triptych of 1950 by his friend Oskar Kokoschka.

It was always implicit in Courtauld's vision of the memorial to his wife that it should engage with the art of the present century. It was therefore particularly welcome when the collection formed by Dr Alistair Hunter (1909–83) mostly in the 1970s was bequeathed to the University. The collection is chiefly distinguished for the series of major works by Ivon Hitchens, an

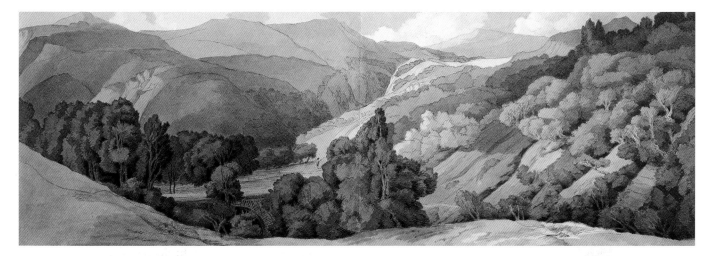

Francis Towne (1740–1816), *Near Devil's Bridge, Central Wales*, watercolour. Spooner Collection.

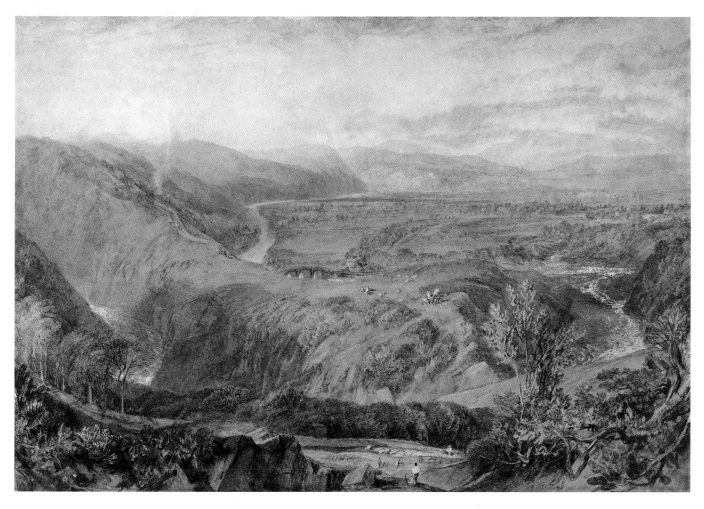

J.M.W. Turner, *The Crook of Lune, looking towards Hornby Castle*, pencil, watercolour and body colour, c.1816–18. Stephen Courtauld bequest.

artist whom Hunter particularly admired, but it contains also British classics such as *Painting 1937* by Ben Nicholson and the study for the Tate Gallery's *Origins of the Land* of 1950 by Graham Sutherland. Like Courtauld, Hunter was essentially an *amateur* of art, with a keen and discriminating eye. Lillian Browse on the other hand was, and happily remains, a thorough professional. One of the first women to break into the charmed masculine circle of the London art trade, she was a key member of the well-known firm Roland, Browse and Delbanco, which dominated sales of contemporary British art to museums throughout the country during the 1950s and 1960s. In the course of her work, Miss Browse built up a personal collection of drawings, paintings and sculptures, including an especially distinguished group of paintings by Walter Sickert, drawings by Henry Moore and bronzes by Degas and Rodin. In 1984 she presented her collection to the University of London for display, after her death, at the Courtauld Gallery.

Despite these generous gifts and bequests, the adequate representation of the art of the twentieth century and beyond remains a challenge for the Gallery. The justice of Courtauld's essential conviction that European art had been renewed through the work of the Impressionists and Post-Impressionists is to some extent belied by the absence of great works of the Fauve or Cubist movements, or major works of German Expressionism or American abstraction. Both for teaching purposes, and to fulfil the character of the displays, it is most desirable that this gap should be filled. The problem is partly one of space, for so much of the most important work by twentieth-century artists has been on a very large scale. More profoundly, it is a question of the Gallery's nature and historic character, as a collection of collections. On that basis it seems necessary to await – but with a confidence based on the experience of the past – further great benefactions to take the Gallery into the new century.

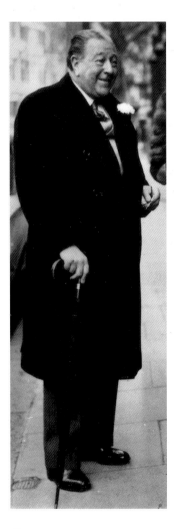

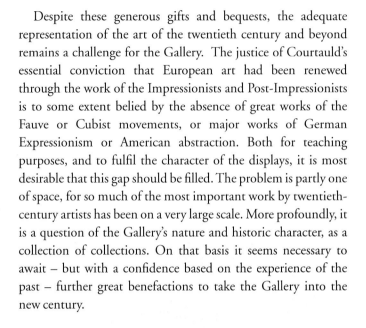

Count Antoine Seilern (1901–78).

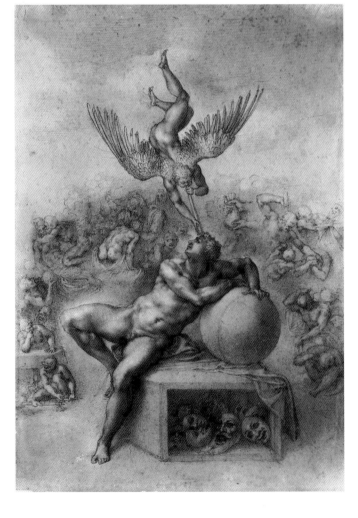

Michelangelo (1475–1546), *The Dream of Human Life*, black chalk (39.6 x 28 cm). Princes Gate Collection.

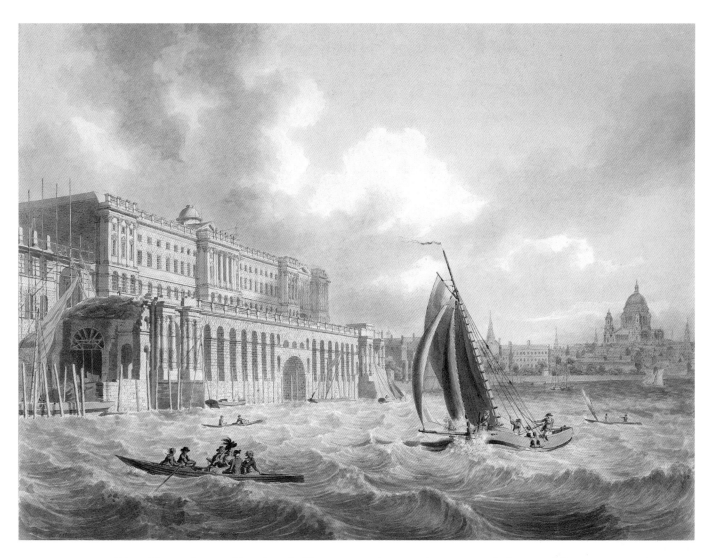

Edward Dayes, *Somerset House from the Thames*, watercolour, 1788 (42.7 x 57.5 cm). Spooner Collection.

The Gallery in Somerset House

Though Samuel Courtauld's intention was that his collection and the great Adam house in Portman Square should together constitute the memorial to his wife, it is now the Courtauld Institute and Gallery which fulfil that role at Somerset House. The move from Portman Square became clearly necessary in the 1980s partly because the house was neither suitable nor large enough for a major teaching institution, partly because the collections had spectacularly outgrown their accommodation in Woburn Square. After a long search it was decided that the North Block of Somerset House, which had been vacated a decade earlier by the Registrar-General of Births, Marriages and Deaths, should be leased from the Crown and converted for the use of all parts of the Institute. Work was completed in 1989, and the libraries and teaching functions of the Institute moved into the East and West wings and the basements during the summer; the Gallery occupied the *corps de logis*, or central portion, the following year.

Somerset House stands on the site of the town-house built in 1547–52 for the Duke of Somerset, the Lord Protector, or regent, during the minority of Edward VI. On Somerset's execution in 1552, the house became Crown property, and served as an occasional royal residence, principally as a dower house for successive Queens, throughout the seventeenth and early eighteenth centuries. By 1774 the house was dilapidated, and in a political climate still dominated by Britain's overseas victories in the Seven Years' War, the decision was taken to demolish the old building and to endow London with a public building expressive of the nation's standing in the world. The new building, for which the architectural responsibility was eventually entrusted to Sir William Chambers, was intended to re-house several departments of Government, especially the Navy Office, and to provide accommodation for the nation's learned societies, the Royal Society (founded 1660) and the Royal Academy (founded 1768), joined later by the Society of Antiquaries (founded 1717).

The site was bounded on the north side by the Strand, in the 1770s one of the grandest streets in the West End of London. To

17

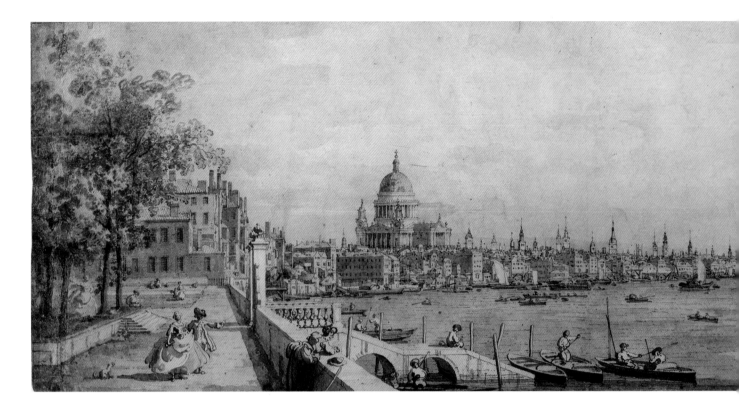

the south, gardens stretched down to a terrace, punctuated by water-gates, which opened on to the tidal beaches of the Thames. The view stretched from the City, dominated by St Paul's Cathedral, to the Palaces of Westminster and Whitehall, around the great curve of the river, with rows of warehouses and busy wharfs on the opposite side. It was a site which had caught the attention of Antonio Canaletto when he had visited London twenty years or so earlier, and which offered the opportunity to express the self-image of Britain as inheritor of the mantle of Venice as the maritime capital of the world.

Chambers prepared himself carefully to meet the challenge, going back through his notebooks of architectural ideas collected on his travels in Italy and France, and revisiting Paris in May 1774 to see the splendid buildings which had gone up since his last visit in 1749. The design on which he eventually settled combines ideas from all these sources, with overt homage to the old palace of Somerset House, in particular its seventeenth-century gallery, then attributed to the father of English Palladianism, Inigo Jones, which faced the river. It is this gallery, with its row of five rusticated arches, which provided him with the answer to the problem of the relatively constricted Strand front, and its relation to the nearby church of St Mary-le-Strand (1714–17) by James Gibbs. Expanding the series of arches to nine, Chambers placed under the three central openings an entrance vestibule which immediately recalls his studies of Italian Renaissance and modern French architecture, and leads beyond into the magnificent central courtyard of the new Somerset House; this sets out the whole structure of the complex for the visitor's comprehension in one *coup d'œil*. On the exterior of

the Strand Block, and throughout the façades of the Courtyard ranges, sculpture and a deliberate variation of the Classical orders allude to the maritime and commercial prospects of the nation, under the just rule of King George III, a statue of whom by John Bacon (1740–99) is the central figure, occupying the most prominent position.

In the Vestibule itself, visitors are informed by inscriptions and by the presence of busts of Michelangelo and Sir Isaac Newton by Joseph Wilton (1722–1803) that they may enter the doors of, respectively, the Royal Academy on the west side (now the entrance to the Gallery) and the Royal Society and Society of Antiquaries on the east (now the entrance to the teaching part of the Courtauld Institute). The interiors, apart from minor variations in plasterwork and the staircase balustrade, are similar on both sides.

The entrance hall which now serves the Gallery was originally crowded with plaster casts of classical sculptures, of which the Furietti Centaurs remain, signifying a welcome to the visitor. The Minerva Giustiniani is also one of the original Academy casts; as the tutelary goddess of learning and the arts, Minerva appears repeatedly in the painted decorations of the whole Academy premises. The hall itself is an open, airy composition, dominated by a Doric screen surmounted by a frieze of lion masks joined by fine swags. To the right are two doors, one of which originally led to the porter's room and to a basement service stair, the other to the first of the Academy's teaching rooms, the Academy of the Living Model. Originally this room (1) was fitted with banked seats and desks, and had a large overhead light which could be shaded to provide interesting shadows

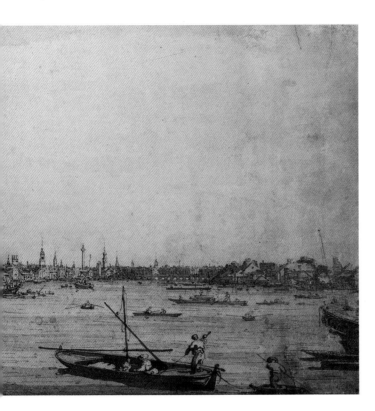

Antonio Canaletto,
A View from Somerset Gardens looking towards London Bridge,
graphite, pen and ink on buff paper, c.1750 (23.5 x 73.2 cm).
Princes Gate Collection.

Below:
Frederick Mackenzie (c.1787–1854),
Porchway, Somerset House,
pencil and watercolour.

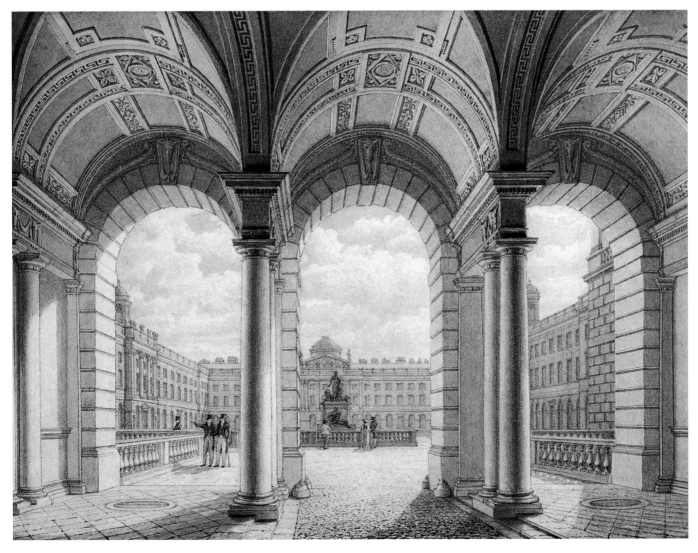

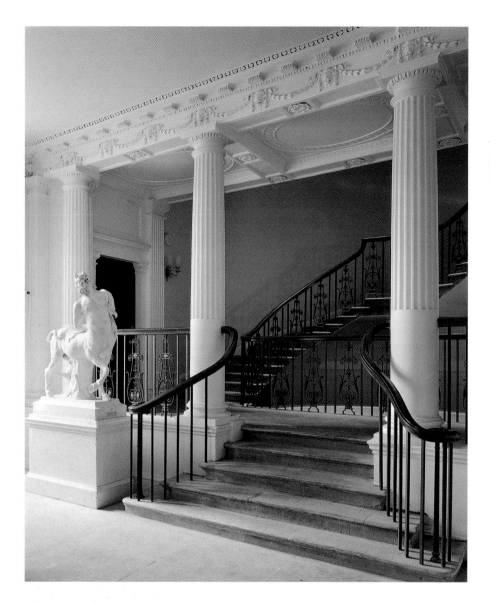

The entrance hall of the Courtauld Gallery, showing the staircase leading to the upper floors.

Opposite:
A meeting of the Royal Society at Somerset House.

across the model's body. Now the upper part is occupied by a mezzanine, and the remaining architecture compromised by a nineteenth-century balcony; in this form, it nevertheless provides a compatible setting for the earliest paintings and other works of art in the Gallery's collection.

The upper part of the Hall provides a view downward into the remarkable basement entrance of an apartment provided for the Keeper of the Royal Academy. Served by a side stair, the area is fully 'dressed' with fictive rusticated stonework executed in wood to give at least some sense of status appropriate to the Academy's senior resident official. It is lit from the skylight of the staircase above, which gives a somewhat 'Piranesian' feel to the basement, similar to that of the courtyard wells outside. However, this same gloom is essential to the drama of the staircase itself, ascending as it does from darkness into light, passing upward through the hierarchy of the Classical orders from Doric to Corinthian, and providing metaphorically an allegory of the progress of the student through the curriculum of the Academy.

When the Academy opened in 1780, the staircase immediately became one of the sights of London. Its steepness – the unavoidable result of Chambers's wish to provide high, grand rooms for the learned societies in a very constricted site – and the daring slenderness of the flights sweeping unsupported around the curved walls, contribute to a sense of vertigo, even of 'terror', which is increased as the visitor pauses to look up or down. The emotion of terror in fact was a key ingredient of the category of aesthetic experience known in the eighteenth century as the Sublime, and there seems little doubt that Chambers used the full resources of his art to achieve it here.

On the first floor, where the architectural order becomes Composite, or Roman, Chambers arranged the main suites of rooms for the learned societies. Now considerably altered to provide a continuous circuit, the suites were originally arranged in two interlocking groups of three rooms. The doors, therefore, between the present rooms 2 and 3 and between rooms 5 and 6 are not part of Chambers's scheme. Rooms 2 and 4 were originally the ante-rooms to the two suites, the latter shared by the

Royal Society and the Society of Antiquaries, the former serving also as the Library of the Academy. Both are richly ornamented, the plasterwork by the master craftsman Thomas Collins (1735–1830), and the paintings by Giovanni Battista Cipriani (1727–85). The ceiling of the Academy ante-room was originally graced by a painting by Sir Joshua Reynolds himself, presenting the *Theory of Painting*; this was removed in the nineteenth century and has been replaced by a copy.

The visitor may pass through the rooms in any sequence, but in order to provide a coherent experience for those who wish primarily to look at paintings, the collection is arranged in an anti-clockwise direction around the circuit of the rooms. Following this progression, therefore, the visitor next enters (3) the former Meeting Room of the Royal Society, originally fitted out

by the cabinet-maker George Seddon (1727–1801) with fixed benches and President's Chair, and walls covered with portraits of the Society's luminaries. The ceiling, which bears a profile of the Society's founding royal patron, King Charles II, is one of Chambers's most noble creations, a coffered design alluding to Renaissance and Baroque antecedents, but lightened with gracefully trailing acanthus leaves around the central oval. It was repainted according to surviving evidence of the original colour-scheme in 1989–90.

Passing through the Society's shared Ante-Room (4), the visitor turns into the first of three large rooms on the north, Strand, side of the building. This is the Meeting Room of the Society of Antiquaries (5), the initial letters of which appear in the fine plaster decoration of the ceiling; here the ground colours

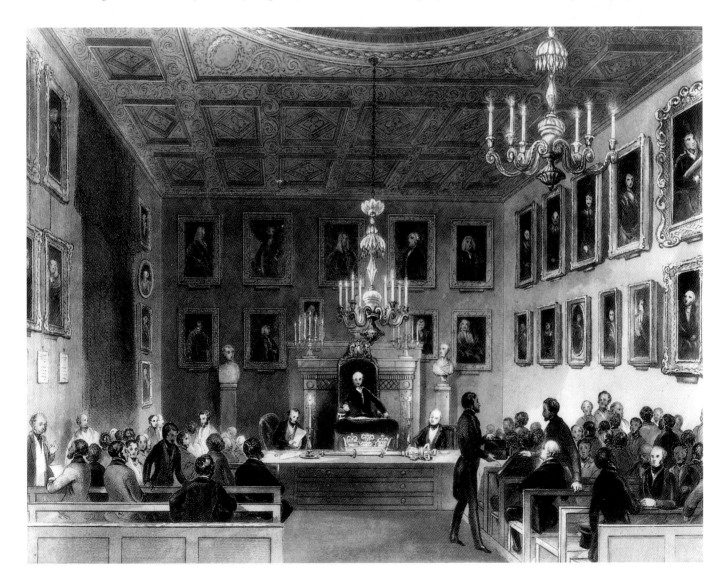

were originally pink and green, the relief ornament being picked out in shades of white with gilded highlights.

In the next room (6), the main Council Room of the Royal Academy premises, the walls were to be hung with paintings by the founding Academicians, together with State portraits of King George III and Queen Charlotte by Reynolds. Chambers himself provided the hanging plan; Benjamin West (1738–1820) provided a roundel for the ceiling on the subject of *The Graces unveiling Nature*, surrounded by quadrants of *The Four Elements* – that is Earth, Air, Fire and Water; Angelica Kauffmann (1741–1807) contributed the four supporting ovals, representing the four elements of art – Invention, Composition, Design and Colouring. All of this painted decoration, together with fireplaces by Joseph Wilton, was stripped out when the Academy moved in 1837, but the plaster ceiling, with its four winged figures, each supported by two lions, trailing swags around and behind the principal paintings, remains as eloquent testimony to the exquisite quality of the original workmanship. It was intended that the relief work should be painted in various shades of white, with gilded highlights, on grounds of green and dove-grey. The ceiling paintings are represented now by tinted photographs of the originals (which can be seen in the entrance hall of the Royal Academy, Burlington House).

The last room on this level (7), the architectural counterpart of 5, originally served both as a subsidiary council chamber, and as the Antique Academy, in which students drew and studied the human form in movement and in the expression of emotion, using casts of Classical and Renaissance sculpture from the Academy's collection. Were it not upstaged by the two principal ceilings on this floor, that of the Antique Academy would attract more attention. Painted in colours *en suite* with the other rooms, the ceiling bears the monogram of the Royal Academy in each corner, and is perhaps specially remarkable for the very fine pierced foliar ornament which runs around it and enlivens its beams and mouldings. Throughout the building, the fineness of detail in the plaster, and indeed of the woodwork, has to a great extent been lost under coats of mostly modern paint, in some places as much as 5 mm in depth. Though something of the glory of the original interiors has been recovered through recent research and skilled redecoration, appreciation of the graceful simplicity of design, coupled with extraordinary attention to finish and detail in the execution, so typical of the building, still requires an act of imagination on the part of the visitor.

Returning to the stairwell, the visitor begins the most formidable part of the ascent, the *Gradus ad Parnassum*, noticing

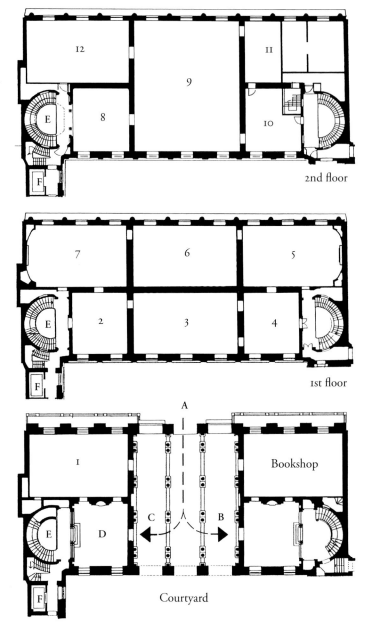

the wide coffered arch with bravura plaster ornament in high relief over the door to the apartments below, and on the curved wall above, a plaster frame that once held a painting by Cipriani showing Minerva visiting the Muses on Parnassus. The ascent of this flight of stairs by crowds of visitors to the annual exhibition of the Academy was famously satirized by Rowlandson in his watercolour and prints of *The Exhibition Stare-case* c.1800. Rowlandson bawdily places a cast of *Venus Callipygia* where a window should be on the staircase, and substitutes a reclining Venus for the scholarly Minerva in the Cipriani painting.

Opposite:
Floor plans of the North Block, showing the rooms (numbered 1 to 12) now occupied by the Courtauld Gallery.

KEY:
A	Entrance to Vestibule from the Strand
B	Entrance to Courtauld Institute teaching departments and administration
C	Entrance to Courtauld Gallery
D	Entrance hall
E	Staircase
F	Lift

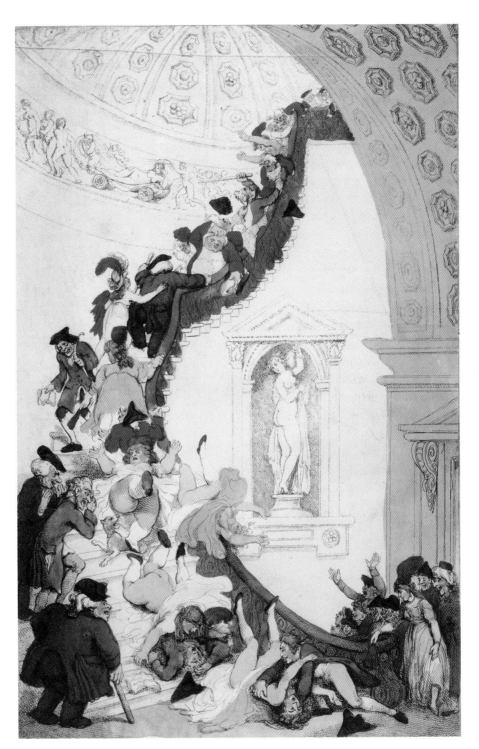

Thomas Rowlandson,
The Exhibition Stare-case, watercolour,
c.1800.

The second floor provides both architecturally and dramatically the climax to the building. Chambers regarded the Corinthian as the highest and most graceful of the Classical orders, and he here greets the visitor with a lovely Corinthian screen, the counterpart of the Doric on the ground floor, on a landing which is literally flooded with light from the sky. This leads to the small and perfect Ante-Room (8), originally decorated in the lunettes over the screen, and over the entrance to the Great Room, with paintings on the theme of the Muses and Parnassus by J.F. Rigaud. Entry to the Great Room itself (9) is signalled by the inscription ΟΥΔΕΙΣ ΑΜΟΥΣΟΣ ΕΙΣΙΤΩ ('Let no one uninspired by the Muses enter here'). The Great Room, designed as an improvement on the Salon Carré of the Palais du Louvre which had since 1737 been used for the annual exhibitions of the Académie Française, was the principal public space of the Royal Academy. Lit by an experimental central lantern, carried by carpentry on the limits of available technology, it was intended to provide the maximum display space with optimum natural lighting, and the largest possible central area for visitors to meet and converse, and to constitute themselves, as we would now say, as a 'Public'. Hugely successful in meeting the latter objective, the room has however always presented problems for the display of paintings. The angles at which the light falls on pictures hung on the upper part of the walls causes reflections in the eye of the spectator, so Chambers had to provide a ledge onto which the bottoms of the frames could be locked, allowing their tops to hang forward and outwards. Paintings thus hung 'on the line' were usually those considered the most important, or at least were the largest, in the Exhibition. As the annual shows increased in size, the 'hang' extended higher and higher, the pictures at the top being regarded as 'skied', or virtually invisible from below. The effect was obviously unfortunate for the artists concerned, but must have been stupendous for the visitor. The display forms the subject of the watercolours by J.H. Ramberg showing the Exhibition of 1787 being visited by the Prince of Wales and other members of the Royal Family.

The role of the Great Room in the public life of London was magnificently realized at such moments.

The other rooms on the second floor (10, 11 and 12) were not originally part of the parade. The doors to rooms 10 and 11 are modern interventions and the rooms themselves, which originally belonged to the private accommodation of the resident officials of the Royal Society and the Antiquaries, have since been very much altered. Room 12 originally contained two floors, joined by a service staircase in the 'spandrel' of the curve of the main stair, and provided accommodation for the housekeeper of the Academy. Subsequently, and possibly in response to early nineteenth-century criticisms that the Academy did not do enough to teach the art of actual painting, the space was adapted to serve as the Painting School. Its raised floor, causing the awkward steps between it and the landing and Great Room, is relatively modern.

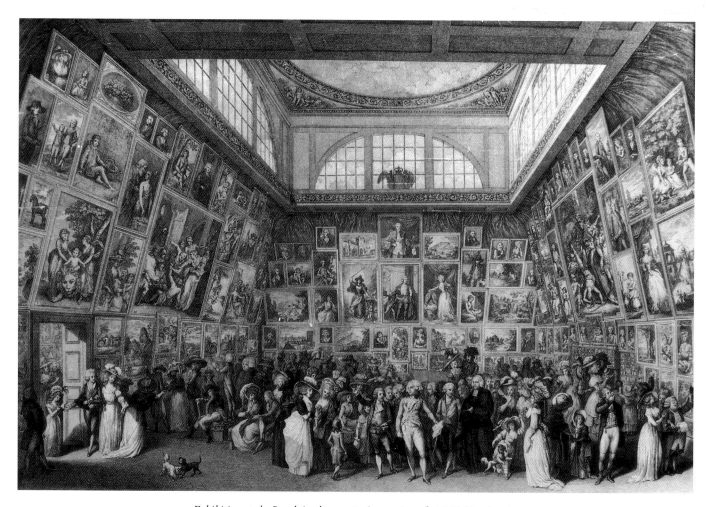

Exhibition at the Royal Academy, 1787 (engraving after J.H. Ramberg).

THE PLATES

The sequence of the works illustrated is broadly chronological, beginning with the Bernardo Daddi triptych of 1338, one of the earliest works in the collection. Where several works by the same artist are reproduced, they are grouped together and the sequence is again chronological; thus, of the five paintings by Rubens included here, *The Descent from the Cross* of 1611, together with the related wings forming a triptych, is placed first, followed by the portrait of Jan Bruegel and his family, and ending with the magnificent late *Landscape by Moonlight* of c.1637–8.

Unless otherwise indicated, a work is unsigned and/or undated. All dimensions are given in centimetres, height before width.

Some of the descriptive notes are reprinted or have been adapted from previous Courtauld Gallery publications, in particular *100 Masterpieces from the Courtauld Institute Galleries* (1987) and *The Princes Gate Collection* (1981), which are now out of print.

The name of the individual collection within the Courtauld Gallery is noted at the end of each entry, followed by the accession number, shown in square brackets.

List of contributors

H.B.   Helen Braham

W.B.   William Bradford

J.C.   Joanna Cannon

D.E.   David Ekserdjian

D.F.   Dennis Farr

J.F.   Jennifer Fletcher

S.G.   Stephen Gritt

C.H.   Colum Hourihane

J.H.   John House

R.H.   Rupert Hodge

S.H.   Sarah Hyde

J.M.   John Murdoch

A.W.-L.   Aidan Weston-Lewis

J.W.   Joanna Woodall

DADDI, BERNARDO   recorded from
1327, died 1348
Triptych:
*The Virgin and Child Enthroned with Saints
and Angels* (centre); *The Redeemer* (above);
*The Nativity, The Crucifixion, The Four
Evangelists, The Annunciation* (inside of
wings); *The Adoration of the Magi, Two
Bishop Saints* (outside of wings)   1338
Tempera on panel. Max. height 87.5; width
at base 42; wings 62 (max.) x 17
Dated on plinth: 'ANNO DNI [M]CCCXXXVIII'

This triptych is an exquisite example of the
type of portable tabernacle produced for
private patrons in fourteenth-century Italy.
Because its physical structure and paint
surface are remarkably well preserved, it is
possible to gauge the work's original effect
and use. Whether standing in the home or
taken on a journey, the triptych could be
opened for prayer and meditations, and
then, when closed again, admired for the
scene which, in this sole surviving example,
is painted on the outside of the shutters.
Long, detailed, and repeated contemplation
of each image was possible. The density
and richness of the tabernacle's surface
decoration, and of its religious content,
rewarded this close attention.

   The surface shimmers with gold.
Burnished and stamped leaf is used to fill the
backgrounds, while filaments of leaf, applied
to the bright egg tempera paint surface,
embellish the undulating hem of the Virgin's
mantle, lend the appearance of rich brocade
to the material of the throne back, or
describe the highlights on the individual
feather of Gabriel's wings. The panel's closely
packed images constitute a compendium of
major Christian truths presented in the form
of detailed narratives. Meditation on the
Nativity, for instance, would be enlivened
by observing the tender communication
between Mother and Child shown here.
Reciprocal glances and gestures recur as a
motif throughout. Gabriel's salutation to the
Virgin and her hesitant response link the
two separate parts of the Annunciation scene
which crown the inner faces of the shutters
on either side of the central panel. On the

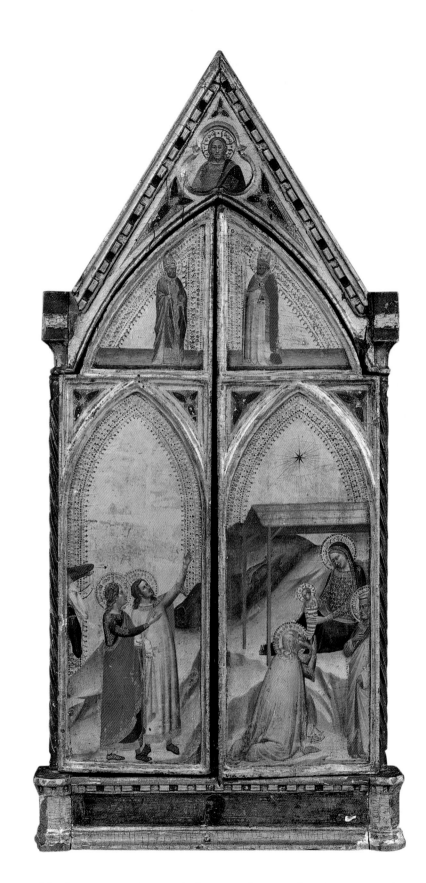

reverse of the shutters are two images which,
when the tabernacle is closed, unite to form
the scene of the Adoration of the Magi. On
the left wing two of the Magi gaze and
gesture towards the star beyond the central
framing moulding. Turning this interruption

to advantage, the artist continues the rocky
landscape beyond the frame, creating the
illusion of a single scene, witnessed through
a pair of arched windows.

   The present triptych is attributed to the
Florentine artist Bernardo Daddi, and the

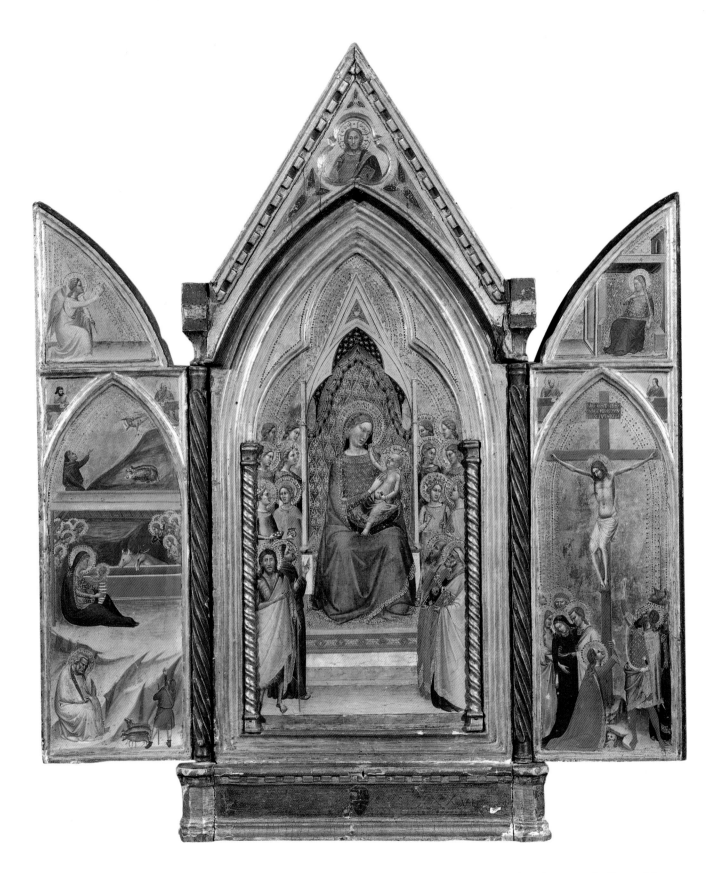

date 1338 falls neatly in the middle of Daddi's known œuvre, since his earliest surviving work is the Ognissanti triptych of 1328, while his last signed and dated work is the S. Giorgio a Ruballa polyptych of 1348, also in the Courtauld collections, painted in the year of his death. Daddi, who felt the influence of both Giotto and of his Sienese contemporaries, appears to have run a well-organized and prolific workshop, specializing in the production of panel paintings, many of them devotional tabernacles. The present triptych ranks among the finest of these works, both in terms of the refinement of its execution and of the quality of its narrative invention. J.C.

Princes Gate Collection [P.1978.PG.81]

MONACO, LORENZO c.1370–c.1425
The Coronation of the Virgin c.1394–5
Tempera on panel in original frame,
208 x 179

The attribution of this painting in 1950 by
Hans Gronau to the young Lorenzo Monaco
is now generally accepted. Gronau identified
the picture as the most substantial, topmost
element of a large, complex altarpiece
painted for the high altar of the Church of
San Gaggio (Caius) in Florence. Four other
fragments of the same altarpiece have also
been identified: two wing panels, one
depicting St Catherine of Alexandria and
the other St Caius (Accademia, Florence),
and two sections of the predella, a *Last
Supper* and a *Martyrdom of St Catherine of
Alexandria* (both in Berlin).

The painting, which also includes *Christ
in Benediction* at the apex, probably dates
from c.1394–5, that is, approximately three
years after Lorenzo Monaco (born Piero di

Giovanni in Siena) was ordained a monk of
the Camaldolensian Order.

Lorenzo's apprenticeship is not
documented, but it is likely that he trained
with both Agnolo Gaddi, the leading
Florentine painter of the period, and also in
the workshop of Jacopo and Nardo di Cioni.
Gaddi's influence is visible in the facial types
of the figures, and also in the use of the
subtle pinks, yellows and greens of the shot
materials of the angels' draperies. Mary's
robe, too, would have been in a similar
sweet and high-key palette, for technological
investigation has shown that when first
painted, it was a tender shade of violet,
made from a mixture of ultramarine and
red lake. However, red lake, a natural dye,
fades on exposure to light.

The influence of the Cioni workshops is
more easily verifiable, for an exact replica of
the bird motif on the rich orange and lapis
lazuli Cloth of Honour is also found in
Nardo di Cioni's *Three Saints* (National

Gallery, London). Nardo used this same bird
motif to decorate areas of brocade in two
altarpieces painted for the monastery of
Santa Maria degli Angeli – the headquarters
of the Camaldolensian order; the bird motif
seen in the present Cloth of Honour was
added by Lorenzo, using the stencil
employed by Nardo di Cioni.

It is not only the rich patterning of the
painted surface which gives this work the
impression of detailed opulence. For in the
gilding of the angels' wings and the haloes –
each one of which is unique – Lorenzo has
used the techniques of punching, engraving,
sgraffito (a technique of scratching through
the paint layer to reveal the underlying gold)
and glazing in order to form texture and
allow the gold to scintillate, while creating
the illusion of depth. W.B.

Gambier-Parry Collection [P.1966.GP.272]

28

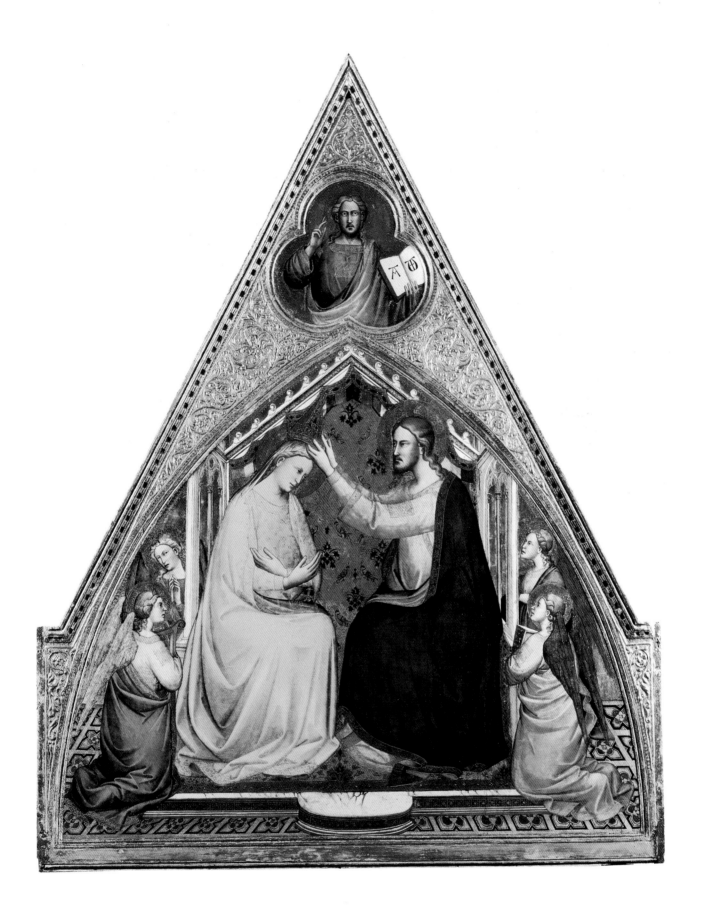

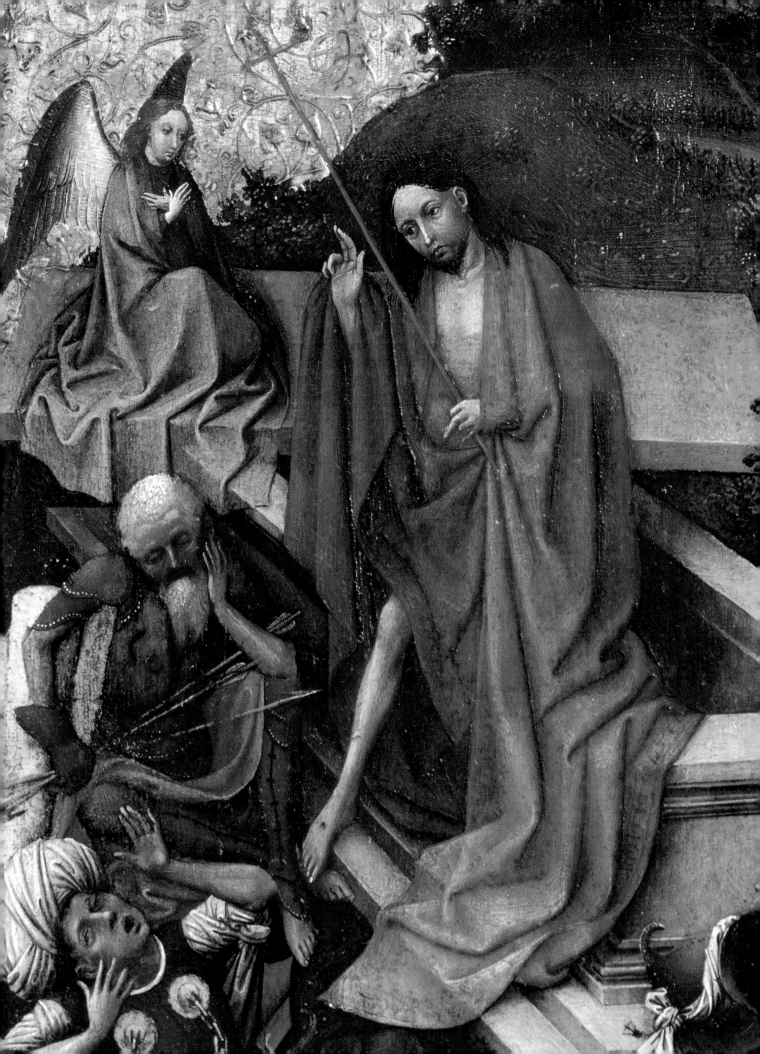

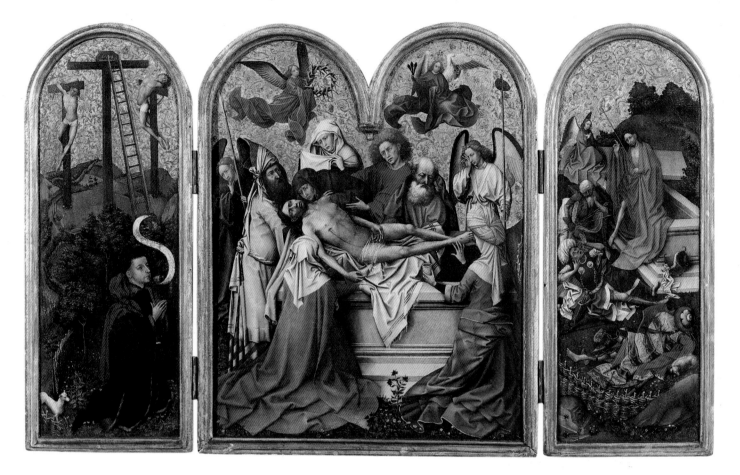

MASTER OF FLÉMALLE
(?Robert Campin) c.1375–1444
Triptych:
The Entombment (centre panel);
*Two Thieves with the Empty Cross and a
Donor; The Resurrection* (wings) c.1420
Panel: centre 60 x 48.9; each wing 60 x 22.5

In the left wing, though Christ's body has
been removed from the central Cross, the
thieves remain in torment on their crosses.
The donor kneels in the foreground; a book
hangs in a cloth cover between his hands; no
trace of an inscription can be found on the
scroll next to his head. In the centre panel,
the body of Christ is lowered into the tomb
by Joseph of Arimathaea and Nicodemus.
The Virgin, supported by St John, leans over
to kiss Christ; the other women are the
Three Marys. Four angels, two hovering
and two standing, carry the Instruments of
the Passion: the spear, Crown of Thorns,

nails and sponge. In the right wing, the
resurrected Christ, watched by an angel,
steps from the tomb, which is guarded by
three soldiers. Two are asleep, while the third
is astonished into consciousness. The boldy
patterned draperies suggest an eastern
setting, and the gilded background, bearing
differing, raised patterns of vine tendrils,
leaves and grapes, relate the subject-matter
to the mysteries of the Eucharist. The frames
are original.

The donor cannot be identified and
nothing is known about the early history of
the triptych. Apparently too small to have
been used as an altarpiece, it may have been
displayed in the donor's home. On stylistic
grounds, the triptych is attributed to the
Master of Flémalle, who painted the panels
of the Virgin and Child and St Veronica
allegedly from Flémalle near Liège and now
at Frankfurt. He was very possibly Robert
Campin, a leading Tournai painter, and the

triptych seems to be his earliest surviving
work. The donor's costume may indicate
that it was painted in about 1420. The artist
has evidently used an oil-based medium,
though one less tractable than that of
Campin's contemporary Jan van Eyck. It has
allowed him to render a wide range of tones
and his boldness in justaposing strongly
constrasting tones and his accuracy in
depicting all the subtle tonal transitions in
the flesh and draperies allow his figures to
appear startlingly convincing. He is able to
reproduce well-defined facial expressions and
dramatically eloquent gestures. The colours,
carefully balanced, and the striking linear
patterns contribute to the powerful
decoration and expressive effect of the
triptych as a whole, which is one of the first
and greatest masterpieces of Early
Netherlandish painting.   W.B.

Princes Gate Collection [P.1978.PG.235]

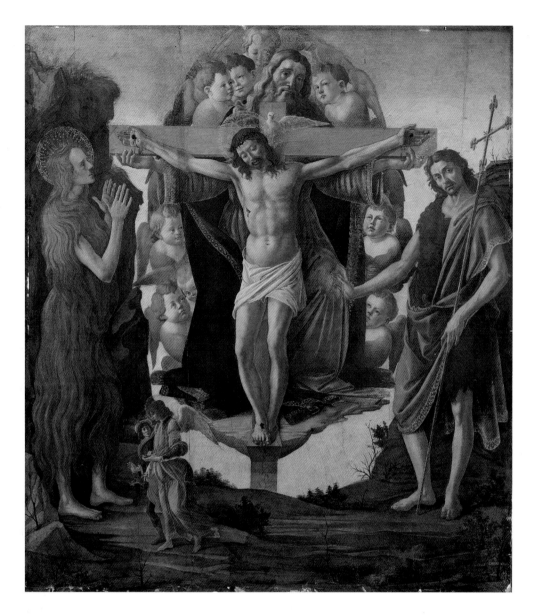

BOTTICELLI (Alessandro Filipepi)
c.1444–1510
*The Trinity with St Mary Magdalen and
St John the Baptist, the Archangel Raphael
and Tobias* c.1491–94
Tempera on panel, 214.9 x 191.2

This is almost certainly the main panel of
the High Altarpiece painted for the
Augustinian Convent of Sant' Elisabetta
delle Convertite in Florence. As part of the
construction of the Convent's new church,
building work on a chapel to contain the
High Altarpiece began in 1491 and was
completed by Christmas 1494. This painting,
which may have been paid for by a lay
patron, was probably executed at this time.
And while it is accepted that its design is the
work of Botticelli, insufficient investigations
have as yet been carried out to determine
how much of the execution is the master's,

and how much may have been the work of
studio assistants.

The Convent of Sant' Elisabetta delle
Convertite was founded in 1329 to house
penitent prostitutes. Its patroness, Mary
Magdalen, is represented on the left of the
Courtauld composition as a penitent, her
unkempt hair resembling a shift of rough
pelts. Balancing this image, on the right, is
the figure of St John the Baptist, the patron
saint of Florence. Both saints stand in an
appropriately barren and rocky landscape.
Raised at the composition's centre is the
Trinity accompanied by cherubim, a motif
known as the Mercy Seat or Throne of
Mercy. While not uncommon in Florentine
art in the closing years of the fifteenth
century, this motif is peculiarly appropriate
to the Convertite.

At the lower left of the composition are
the small figures of Tobias and the Angel,

whose presence cannot be satisfactorily
explained; they may, however, refer to the
guidance and apprenticing of the illegitimate
children of the Convertite. It has been
suggested that these figures were later
additions, included at the behest of the
altarpiece's patron. However, they mesh so
completely into the picture's overall design –
the uneven terrain upon which the larger
figures of the saints stand even becomes for
Tobias and Raphael an arid land of stunted
bushes and rocky outcrops – that this seems
implausible.

Connected with the Trinity are four
predella panels (small-scale panels fitted
below the principal panel of the altarpiece)
depicting the life of Mary Magdalen, in the
John G. Johnson Collection, Philadelphia
Museum of Art.   W.B./D.E.

Lee Collection [P.1947.LF.38]

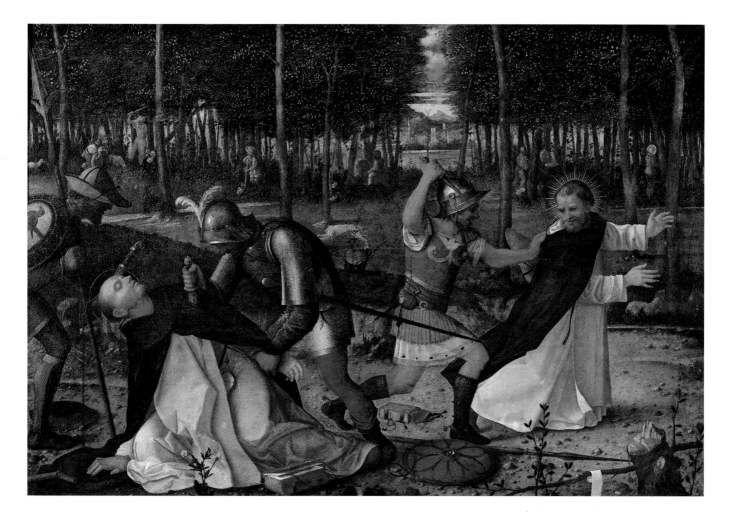

BELLINI, GIOVANNI (ascribed to)
c.1430–1516
The Assassination of St Peter Martyr 1509(?)
Oil on panel, 67.3 x 100.4

This work is attributed to Giovanni Bellini because it closely resembles another version of the subject ascribed to him (National Gallery, London). It is impossible to confirm the date 1509 that is reported to have been visible on the back of the panel, as this is now covered. The original function and location are unknown since the picture was first recorded with a Viennese dealer as recently as 1910, but its size and exquisite detail tend to indicate a close-up view in a connoisseur's collection or some Dominican Prior's cell. A clue to the patron's identity may be found in the arms (a suitably cruel bird of prey) on the soldier's shield. This soldier is significantly absent from the National Gallery painting and, as he is superfluous to the story and the action, his role and striped stockings are probably heraldic. Devotion to Peter Martyr was strong in the Veneto (his birthplace was Verona). In Venice a lay confraternity

propagated his cult by commissioning pictures of his martyrdom. By the early sixteenth century the city owned several parts of his body; the depiction of bleeding trees could relate to a relic of his blood.

The story is told in the Golden Legend. In 1252 the Dominican saint was ambushed between Como and Milan by assassins hired by local heretics. Peter's companion, Brother Dominic, though mortally wounded, managed to escape. Peter, brought to his knees by an axe blow to the head, was stabbed with a dagger; dying, he reaffirmed his Christian belief by writing 'credo' with his blood in the dust. The painter has added telling details: the violent action is paralleled by that of woodmen felling trees, which bleed in sympathy; the buttercup(?) seen blooming prominently in the foreground may be inspired by those flowers in Ovid's *Metamorphoses* which spring from the blood of dying youths loved by the gods and so guarantee their immortality.

The picture is executed on two wooden panels which have split, causing damage horizontally across the centre. The paint is applied thinly with small strokes from fine

brushes, and extensive finger printing suggests some working by hand towards a softer focus. Infra-red examination has revealed many 'pentimenti', notably the widening of the central gap in the trees and the suppression of a small man standing there beside a horse. The tree-trunks were painted in first and show through all the foreground figures except for the left-hand soldier. There are no substantial alterations to those four figures which so closely resemble the principal characters in the National Gallery picture; this – together with the possibility that the wood in the present painting may also once have been continuous – makes it highly likely that the painter was working, under Bellini's supervision, from his master's picture and rearranged its main elements, enlarged the figure scale, invented a soldier and added details like the books, spurs, hound and fallen shield. The result is a painting of very high quality, in which the relationship between figure and landscape is less subtle than in a Bellini but more sensational.   J.F.

Lee Collection [P.1947.LF.29]

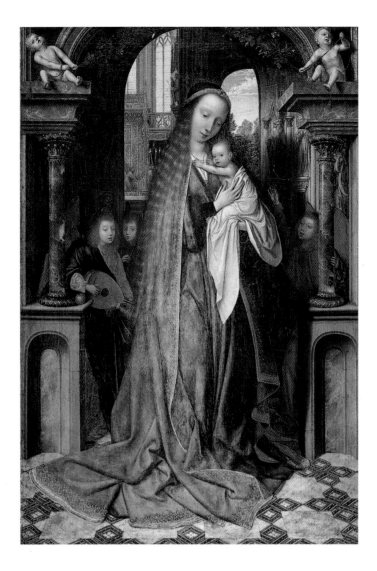

MASSYS, QUINTEN 1466–1530
The Madonna Standing with the Child and Angels c.1500–9
Oil on panel, 47.5 x 33

Few contemporary references to Massys' early career as an artist exist, apart from the fact that he entered the St Luke Guild of Painters in Antwerp in 1491. This city was to remain his home, with the exception of a possible visit or visits to Italy, until his death.

His earliest works, dated to c.1491–1507, are small iconic images of various saints and representations of the Madonna and Child, such as the example in the National Gallery, London. The two commissions for the *St Anne Altarpiece* (1507–9; Brussels, Musées Royaux des Beaux-Arts) and the *St John Altarpiece* (1508–11; Antwerp, Koninklijk Museum) not only constitute a turning point in his career, but also reflect a change in iconography.

With the possible exception of this *Madonna and Child*, Massys was to forsake the earlier and standard iconic image until the last decade of his career. Nothing is known of the original ownership of this work or of the copy now in the Lyons Museum, but it is generally agreed that the present example is the earliest and that it was probably painted between 1500 and 1509 for a wealthy donor or private workshop. Cult images of the Madonna were popular in the fifteenth and sixteenth centuries in the Netherlands, and Massys borrows significantly from such precedents. Whereas Massys' central positioning of the Madonna and Child beneath a vestibule arch is given an Italianate element by the presence of putti with garlands and swags, features which echo the work of Hans Memling, his architectural context is paralleled in a simplified format in the early fifteenth-century work of Jan van Eyck and Robert Campin. Massys' distorted use of perspective is matched by his equally unusual positioning of portal figures representing Old Testament prophets, in a context in which they would never be found in reality. Similarly, the wooded landscape, seen immediately behind the Madonna's head on the right-hand side, is an unlikely element, the basis for which lies in the artist's innovative style. Another element borrowed from van Eyck and Campin is the angelic support to the Madonna. Here, one angel is shown playing a lute, another with a possibly bowed instrument, a third offering a flower and yet another in the background preparing a throne, the canopy of which carries an inscription '. . . us' and 'Maria'. The emphasis throughout the picture – from the finely painted halo to the lofty architectural setting, the attendant angels and the preparation of the throne – is on the majesty of the Madonna.

Another example of this artist's work in the Princes Gate Collection is *Christ on the Cross, between the Virgin, St John and Two Donors*, dating to the early 1490s.   C.H.

Princes Gate Collection [P.1978.PG.245]

34

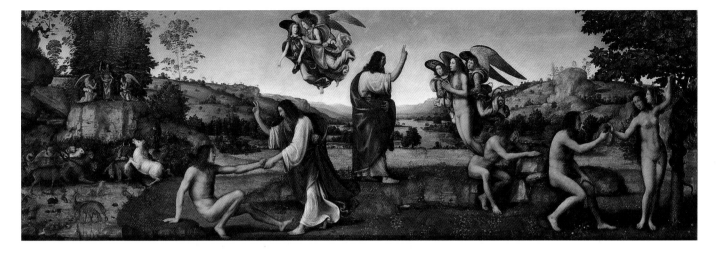

ALBERTINELLI, MARIOTTO
1474–1515
The Creation c.1513–15
Oil on panel, 56.5 x 165.5

The Creation is one of two panels of comparable height by Albertinelli depicting scenes from the book of Genesis. The second painting, formerly in the Strossmayr collection, Zagreb, shows the *Expulsion from Paradise*; this design is incomplete, and seems to have been cut down at the right. The Courtauld and Zagreb paintings are identical in style, as are the figure-scale and emphasis of the landscape background, and may possibly be identified as two of the three little narrative pictures (*tre storiette*) said by the historian Giorgio Vasari to have been painted for the Florentine Giovanni Maria Benintendi, after the election of Leo X as Pope. This election took place in 1513, but it is possible that *The Creation* was not completed until some two years later.

The long, low format common to both the Courtauld and the Zagreb pictures suggests that they were either intended for the decoration of a *cassone* – a chest in which wedding linen was stored – or a similar item of furniture.

As frequently happened with *cassone* painting, *The Creation* observes the convention of representing a number of moments from a single narrative in the same pictorial area. The episodes are arranged chronologically, from left to right. In the Creation of the Animals, in the left background, Albertinelli's exotic creatures recall those in Piero di Cosimo's earlier work, for example the painting *Forest Fire* (Ashmolean Museum, Oxford), while the rearing horse is reminiscent of those in the early drawings of Leonardo da Vinci. Next is the Creation of Adam, in which Adam rises to his feet with the aid of God the Father, who makes the sign of blessing over him. At the centre of the panel Eve is created from

the rib of the slumbering Adam; and finally, closing the right of the composition, the Temptation and Fall. Here, Eve offers Adam not an apple, but a split fig from the laden tree, while the human-headed serpent, curled around the trunk, whispers encouragement in her ear.

The figures in the Creation and Fall of Mankind, whose poses often refer to those found in ancient statuary or reliefs, are disposed in a shallow arc on a stage-like grassy bank in the foreground. To unify the elements of the Creation story, and in order to lend depth to the painting, Albertinelli constructs a landscape featuring rolling hills and gentle mountains, bisected at the centre of the composition by a broad river flowing into deep space. This placid and luminous landscape derives principally from Flemish paintings by Hugo van der Goes and Hans Memling. W.B.

Gambier-Parry Collection [P.1966.GP.6]

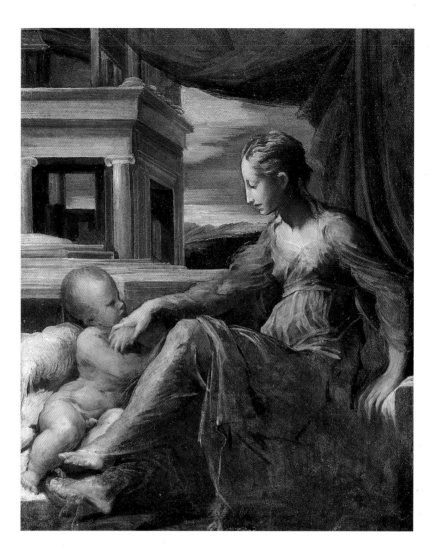

PARMIGIANINO (Girolamo Francesco
Maria Mazzola) 1503–40
The Virgin and Child c.1524–7
Oil on panel, 63.5 x 50.7

The Virgin and Child has generally been
dated to Parmigianino's stay in Rome from
1524 to 1527. Indeed, the classical building in
the background appears to be an evocation
of one of the sights of ancient Rome, the
Septizonium, an impressive ruin
subsequently demolished in 1588; the same
background appears later in a drawing of
The Visitation. The pose of the Virgin may
well have been inspired by the figure of the
Erythraean Sibyl in one of the great modern
sights of Rome, Michelangelo's ceiling in the
Sistine Chapel. Above all, we see here,
succeeding to the Correggesque charm of the
artist's early work, the gravity of the art of
Raphael, who had died in Rome four years
before Parmigianino's arrival. It was with
Raphael's pupils and artistic circle that the
young artist was particularly associated in
these years; the impact on his art was

profound. His biographer, Vasari, was to
write: 'The spirit of Raphael was said
afterwards to have passed into the body of
Francesco.'

This painting is unfinished and therefore
gives an intimate view of Parmigianino at
work. The artist has completed the
background architecture and brilliant blue
sky with a freedom of handling which
distinguishes it from the earlier *Holy Family*,
also in the Courtauld Gallery. Comparison
of the X-rays of the two paintings shows,
however, that the underlying blocking-in of
the composition is as broadly handled there
as it is here. The curtain must be almost
finished; to the Virgin and Child the
finishing touches were still to come, while
the intended blue of the Virgin's mantle can
only be guessed at; the still-exposed dark
brown ground fills the right corner. Most
interestingly, Parmigianino has left unsolved
the arrangement of the Virgin's legs; both
were evidently first intended to be shown
outstretched, as seen in a preparatory
drawing (Albertina, Vienna), which the

painting follows closely, except for the
presence there of an angel. Two visible
attempts to position the right leg more
supportively in an upright position evidently
did not satisfy the artist either.

The unfinished state of the present
painting may be due to the artist's flight to
Bologna after the Sack of Rome. It was in
Bologna that Vasari bought an unfinished
painting of a Madonna by Parmigianino
that may be the present work. The artist
spent the last ten years of his life mainly in
Parma, where he apparently became
increasingly eccentric and absorbed in
hermeticism and alchemy. The contrived
elegance evident in *The Virgin and Child* was
to be pursued almost to bizarre abstraction
in the artist's quest for a personal ideal
beauty. His perfectionism led him to
procrastinate to such a degree that he was
imprisoned for breach of contract. He
escaped and died in exile at the same early
age as Raphael. H.B.

Princes Gate Collection [P.1978.PG.309]

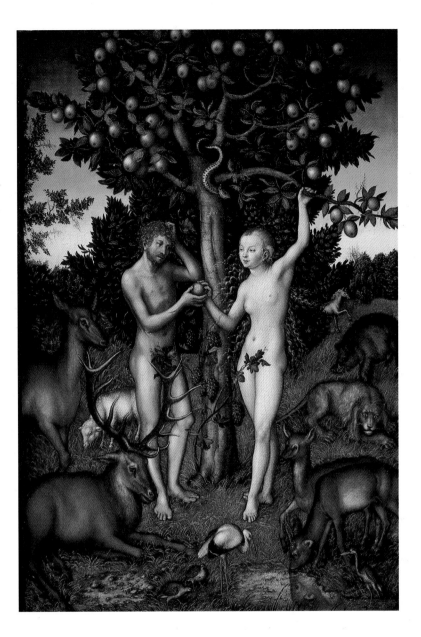

CRANACH, LUCAS, THE ELDER
1472–1553
Adam and Eve 1526
Oil on panel, 117.1 x 80.5
Signed with the winged serpent and dated
1526 on the tree in the centre

The animals in the Garden of Eden are a stag, a hind, a sheep, a roe-buck, its head reflected in the pool, with its mate, a lion, a wild boar and a horse; the birds are partridges, a stork and a heron. Silhouetted against another tree behind is the Tree of Knowledge. Around its trunk a grape-vine grows and from its branches the Serpent emerges to tempt Eve, who is shown offering the apple to the perplexed Adam. On the tree-trunk are the date 1526 and the bat-winged serpent which formed part of Cranach's coat of arms.

Cranach, who was a close friend of Martin Luther, worked at the court of Saxony. The artist, who was famous for his landscapes, his representations of animals and his nudes, found in Adam and Eve a subject which was ideally suited to his gifts and to which the Lutherans did not object. He and his workshop treated it many times in paintings and prints.

This painting is influenced by Dürer's celebrated engravings of the same subject, dated 1504. Dürer had also included many animals but, while Dürer's animals may be interpreted as allusions to the Four Humours, Cranach's animals are less solemn and portentous. A related drawing once at Dresden, though closer to Dürer's print, is still less solemn than the painting; there Eve puts the apple in Adam's mouth and Adam holds a phallic apple-branch which both

conceals and connects his and Eve's genital organs. The vine, not present in the drawing, refers to the Redemption, so that the picture has some didactic function. While the pairing of the sheep with the lion may have a moral meaning, the association of Adam with the sheep is perhaps intended as a wry comment on his behaviour. The principal purpose of the painting, which was presumably made for a wealthy collector, is evidently to give pleasure rather than instruction. Cranach holds a balance between highly decorative, stylized forms and an immediacy and liveliness of presentation. The unexpectedly free technique of the foliage and grass is a reminder that Cranach was renowned for his speed of working.   W.B.

Lee Collection [P.1947.LF.77]

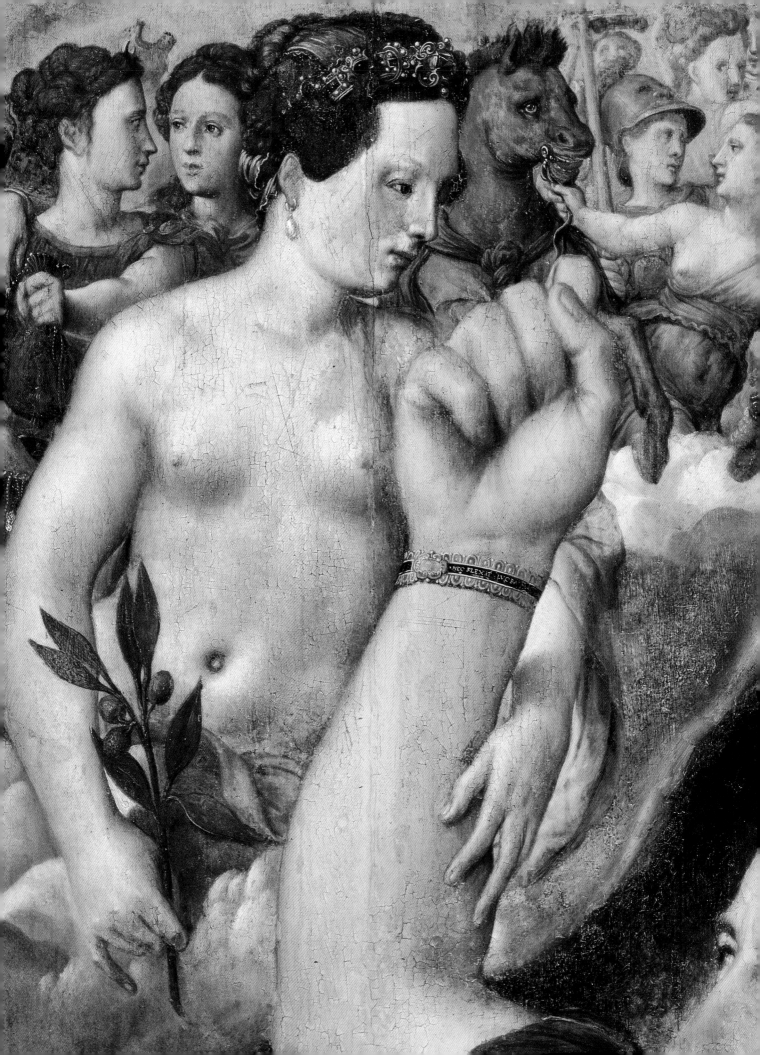

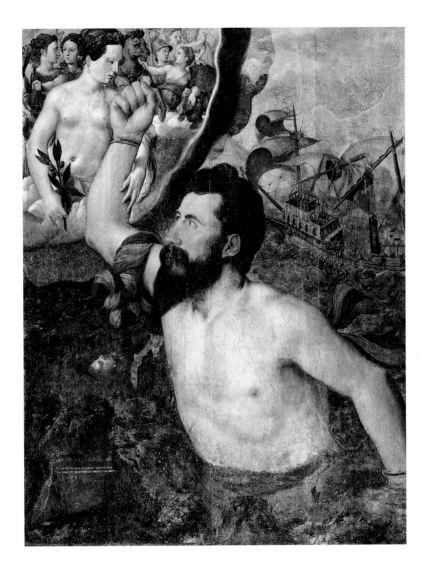

EWORTH, HANS c.1520–c.1574
Allegorical Portrait of Sir John Luttrell
Oil on panel, 109.3 x 83.8
Signed with monogram, 'HE', and dated 1550

Little is known about the painter of this enigmatic portrait, despite the fact that he painted for Mary Tudor and Elizabeth I. 'Eworth' is an anglicized Netherlandish name, and it seems that the artist was in Antwerp in the 1540s. He was a Protestant, and may have left Antwerp because of accusations of heresy. In any event, like many Protestant artisans, he came to London, becoming a denizen in 1550. His initial residence, in common with that of many immigrants, was Southwark – just across the river from the current site of the Courtauld Institute – where he could work outside local guild restrictions.

Eworth's surviving work consists mainly of painted portraits, of which that of Sir John Luttrell is the most exciting and intriguing example, demonstrating a versatility we might expect from a painter trained in a Northern Mannerist tradition. This conjunction of levels of representation is unique in English portraiture at this time.

In brief, the painting celebrates the peace between England and France resulting from the Treaty of Boulogne (24 March 1550), and the significance that it had for Sir John personally. One condition of this Treaty was that English forces withdraw from Scotland, and for Sir John, an army Captain who had been posted on Inchcolm Island in the Firth of Forth for three years and held prisoner, this meant a welcome return home.

The painting depicts Sir John, steadfast in a heavy sea. Behind him, a ship is blasted by lightning, and panic-stricken sailors leap into the water, where they drown. This perhaps refers to Sir John's experience aboard the *Mary Hamborough*, which was caught in a storm, but perhaps also more generally symbolizes outrageous fortune, throwing Sir John's very evident strengths of endurance into sharp relief. This sentiment is echoed in a couplet inscribed on a rock in the foreground, penned by Sir John himself:

More then the rock amyddys ye raging seas
The constant heart no danger dreaddys nor fearys

Bringing comfort, with a reassuring touch, is the allegorical figure of Peace, holding the olive branch. Sir John's devotion is shown by his wearing of her colours, and inscriptions on bracelets testify to his character. Around her are figures from Classical mythology common to allegories of peace, but interestingly, we see depicted a specific term of the Treaty of Boulogne: that France repay monies borrowed from Henry VIII, in two instalments. Eworth shows the goddess Diana, with the crescent moon at her forehead, also the symbol of Henry II of France, holding out a purse and reaching with her other hand for the second instalment.   S.G.

Lee Collection [P.1947.LF.119]

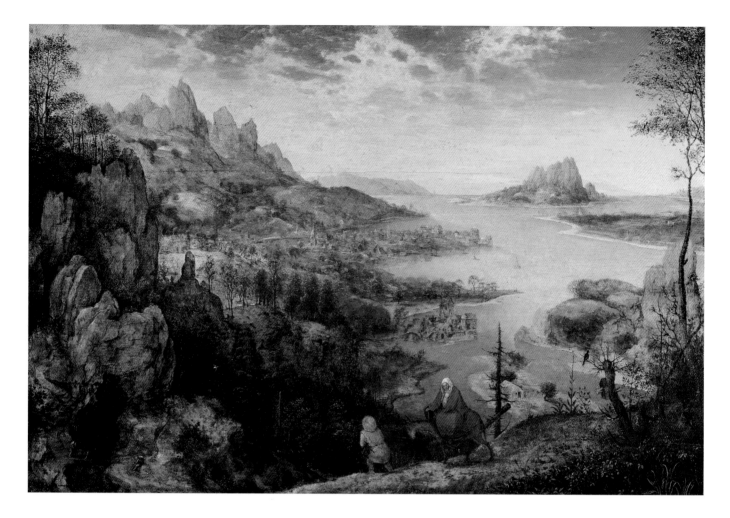

BRUEGEL, PIETER, THE ELDER
c.1525–1569
Landscape with the Flight into Egypt 1563
Oil on panel, 37.1 x 55.6
Signed lower right and dated 'MDLXIII'

Bruegel painted this work soon after his arrival in Brussels, apparently for Antoine Perrenot de Granvella, then Archbishop of Malines. However, the only existing record of the picture in Granvella's collection is in an inventory of 1607 detailing the contents of his house at Besançon.

The painting may be seen as the culmination of a series of landscape drawings that Bruegel had made while journeying through Switzerland to Italy a decade earlier; and the artist is now thought to have continued making similar, imaginary, drawings of Alpine scenery on his return to the Netherlands. In this work, however, he adheres to landscape conventions formulated by an earlier generation of Northern painters. For

although Bruegel's landscape-construction is here more sophisticated, with individual details of foliage and flowers more acutely rendered, the mountainous, riverine panorama observed from an elevated viewpoint nevertheless recalls the *Weltlandschaft* (literally 'world landscape') paintings created by Netherlandish and German artists at the turn of the sixteenth century. The bands of colour by which Bruegel suggests aerial perspective and unifies the landscape – brown in the foreground, green in the middle distance, and grey-blue for the background – although now subtly blended into each other, continue the convention formulated by such Antwerp artists as Joachim Patinir, Herri met de Bles, or Cornelis Massys. In the celebrated series of five paintings, *The Months,* executed only two years after the present work, Bruegel abandoned this tripartite colour division of landscape.

Bruegel's interest here is primarily in the landscape, yet the plight of the Holy Family

on its journey is sympathetically and subtly treated. The quiet drama and urgency of the Flight are indicated by the bent back of Joseph as he tugs on the halter of the stubborn donkey in order to encourage it as they descend a steep slope. The (traditionally) red cloak enveloping Mary, and partly shielding the Christ child at her bosom, suggests the arduous nature of the journey still to come. At the extreme right of the painting, behind the fleeing parents, an idol falls from a willow-trunk, symbolizing the defeat of paganism by the coming of Christ; and in the foreground, by the side of the Holy Family – and on the picture surface, below their feet – crawl two minuscule salamanders, representing Evil.

In the seventeenth century this painting belonged to the two most assiduous collectors of Bruegel's work in Antwerp, first to Rubens, and following his death, to Pieter Stevens.   W.B.

Princes Gate Collection [P.1978.PG.47]

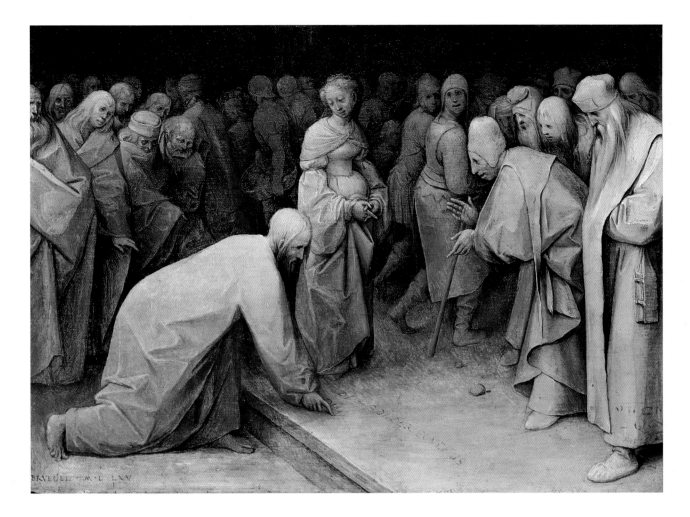

BRUEGEL, PIETER, THE ELDER
c.1525–1569
Christ and the Woman taken in Adultery
1565
Panel, 24.1 x 34.4
Signed and dated, lower left
'BRVEGEL.M.D.LXV'; the inscription on the
ground reads 'DIE SONDER SONDE IS / DIE'
(Flemish text, John, VIII, 7: 'He that is
without sin among you, let him [first cast
a stone at her]')

Along all four edges are prick marks at
regular intervals apparently made with a
compass point to aid the engraver, Paul
Perret (engraving of 1579, not reversed).

Grisaille paintings are rare among
Bruegel's works: *The Death of the Virgin* at
Upton House in Warwickshire (National
Trust) is the most notable other example.
The subject appears to signify a deeply felt
plea for religious tolerance; the artist kept
this painting for himself and it was
apparently the only one inherited by his son,
Jan Bruegel the Elder. The iconographic

scheme is Flemish, but the austere
composition and monumental figures are
perhaps the most Italianate in all Bruegel's
paintings. A copy in Bergamo (Galleria
dell' Accademia Carrara) could be the one
made for Cardinal Federigo Borromeo when
he returned the grisaille to the Bruegel
family; there are a number of copies
attributed to, or by, Jan Bruegel and Pieter
Bruegel the Younger, some in colour and
apparently made from the engraving.

Princes Gate Collection (1981) [P.1978.PG.48]

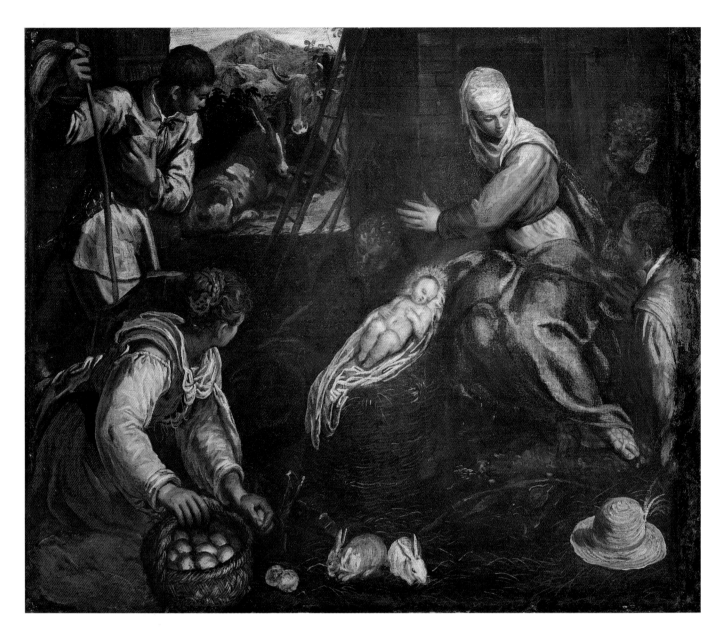

TINTORETTO, JACOPO and/or
DOMENICO 1519–94, and 1560–1635
The Adoration of the Shepherds c.1578
Oil on canvas, 76 x 86.8

Jacopo Robusti, called Tintoretto in allusion
to his father's profession of cloth-dyeing, was
the most prolific painter in Venice in the
sixteenth century. Famous for his rapid,
broken style and unconventional palette, he
has been regarded, especially in England, as
an *enfant terrible* who questioned prevailing
attitudes in society as much as in painting.
He was nonetheless a solid citizen of the
Republic of Venice and a loyal servant of
the secular power, as well as of the leading
charitable confraternities, for which he
carried out brilliant decorative schemes.
Domenico, his elder son, was the leading
assistant in the family studio, and, according

to some scholars, may have been involved
in the production of the present painting.

On this basis, the painting would relate
primarily to the famous treatment of the
subject in 1578 by Jacopo in the Upper
Chamber of the Scuola Grande di S. Rocco
in Venice, on which Domenico also may
have worked. In the Scuola painting, the
Holy Family with two shepherdesses occupy
the upper floor of the stable, with shepherds
and animals in the lower part. Our painting
is, however, a simpler and less innovative
composition, not divided into 'storeys', and
more similar in conception, staffage and
gestural vocabulary to earlier treatments of
the subject by Jacopo (Prague, Castle
Museum, c.1543–4; Verona, Museo di
Castelvecchio, c.1550). These paintings also
include the gift to the Child, by one of the
shepherdesses, of what appear to be eggs.

That a peasant visitor should make such
an offering is inherently credible, but the
gesture also suggests a symbolic significance
beyond the normal iconography of the
Nativity. In some early traditions, Mary is
delivered of the Child without the normal
physical labour. Instead, the Child is
'discovered' lying purely on a patch of straw
beside her. Naturalistic images such as this
seem to translate ideas of the virgin birth
into symbols, so that unassisted, non-uterine
birth is suggested imaginatively by the egg,
which is sometimes also shown lying on
straw or, as here, is given to the Child
directly. Similarly, the egg comes to represent
the idea of Christ's entombment and
resurrection, again acting as a symbol of
Christ's role as Saviour.   J.M.

Princes Gate Collection [P.1978.PG.460]

42

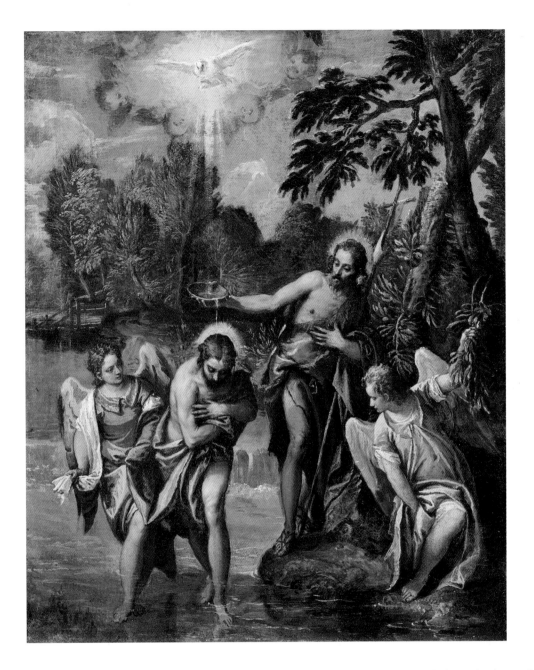

VERONESE (Paolo Calliari)
1528–88
The Baptism of Christ 1580–8
Oil on canvas, 54.8 x 45.6

Veronese's most famous works, enormous frescoes and canvases of religious or mythological subjects, celebrate the power and wealth of Venice at the height of its fortunes. Generally painted for churches or public buildings, they display all the richness of colour for which Venetian painting became renowned throughout Europe.

In the present small picture Veronese reconsiders a subject which he had first treated in important commissions nearly thirty years earlier (paintings now in the Herzog Anton Ulrich Museum, Brunswick,

and the North Carolina Museum of Art, Raleigh), and to which he later returned from time to time, for example in fulfilling a commission for the Sacristy of the Church of the Redentore, Venice, in the 1560s, and again in increasingly powerful renderings (Pitti Palace, Florence, and J. Paul Getty Museum, Malibu, California).

All these compositions have a strong family resemblance, particularly in the stooping attitude of Christ, with his graceful gesture of mingled reverence for the Holy Spirit (the Dove) and acknowledgment of John the Baptist's recognition of his divinity. Exceptionally, the Baptist's sudden awe is expressed here in his instinctive drawing back from Christ, a psychologically convincing gesture which relates to the

solicitude shown by the angels as they observe the human form of Jesus weighed down, as it were, by the Spirit.

The imaginative intensity of the action is reinforced at all levels by the setting. A supernatural light illuminates the figure group, like actors on a stage, emphasizing the extraordinary nature of the event in an otherwise normal world. In the background, the light of early evening is reflected off the still water onto trees, and a sluice-gate indicates an inhabited human landscape. The water is clear and the feet of Christ and the angel are visible through the ripples: both angels clutch their robes to keep them from getting wet.   J.M.

Lee Collection [P.1947.LF.476]

43

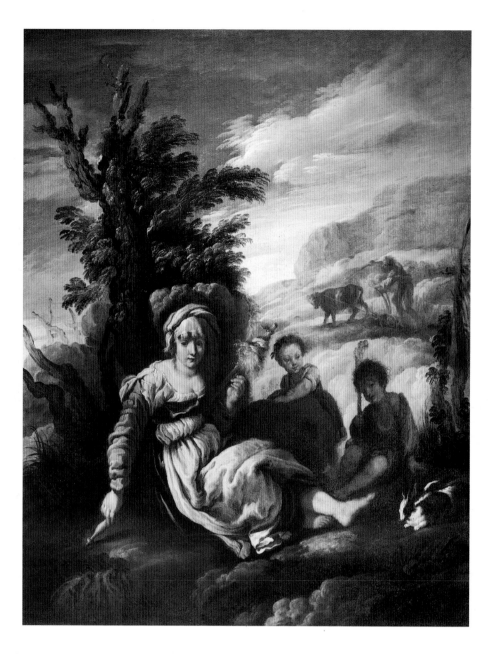

FETTI, DOMENICO 1588/89–1623
Adam and Eve at Work c.1618–20
Oil on panel, 80 x 67.7

Domenico Fetti had a short, meteoric career, from his appointment as Court Painter to Ferdinando Gonzaga, Duke of Mantua, in 1613, until his sudden death in Venice on 16 April 1623. The brilliant era of patronage and collecting by the Gonzaga family came to an end with the death of Ferdinando in 1626 and that of his brother Vincenzo in 1627. The great collections were mostly sold in 1627 to Charles I of Britain; the fifteen works by Fetti were among the King's favourites, combining the rich colour and expressive brushwork of Venetian art with the moral force of the Counter-Reformation's treatment of biblical subjects.

Fetti's most famous paintings in the latter idiom are the series illustrating the Parables of Jesus, commissioned by the Duke of Mantua and executed between 1618 and 1621; the *Parable of the Sower*, acquired by the Duke of Buckingham by 1628, is in the Courtauld Gallery. The present painting, listed in the Gonzaga inventory of 1627 as 'Eve Spinning', passed into the collection of Philip, Duke of Orleans, which was acquired by a syndicate of British connoisseurs in 1798.

The Old Testament subject of *Adam and Eve at Work* is, like a parable, interpreted by Fetti as a representation of a great truth taking place in a normal environment. Eve is depicted as a young wife from the Italian countryside, accompanied by her sons, Cain and Abel, and Adam is shown fulfilling

God's decree 'to till the ground from whence he was taken' (Genesis III, 23). The activity of spinning, also associated with the classical Fates who spin out the unalterable destiny of mankind, refers back to Eve's role in the Fall and Expulsion from Eden, and forward to the murder of Abel by Cain.

Adam and Eve at Work is a rare departure from the predominant Pastoral mode of seventeenth-century landscape painting, in which the figures enjoy primal bliss. In both classical and Christian traditions, work in the landscape signifies the fate of Man after the golden age of innocence. Fetti employed this double resonance to give added moral point to the story as found in Genesis.   J.M.

Presented in memory of Tancred Borenius
[P.1950.XX.123]

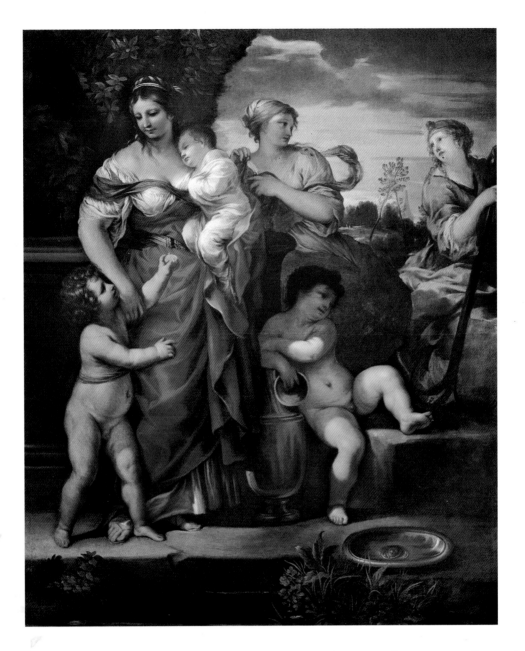

PIETRO DA CORTONA 1596–1669
Faith, Hope and Charity c.1640
Oil on canvas, 171.5 x 128.5 cm (including
a strip of canvas across the top added later).

Pietro Berretini da Cortona was the artist
who, with GianLorenzo Bernini, most fully
expressed the self-confidence of Rome and
the Papacy as a great secular power in
Europe in the mid-seventeenth century.
He worked principally for the Barberini,
one of the dynasties which dominated
political affairs in Rome and which, by
collecting ancient and modern art, made
the city into the artistic capital of the world.
The Barberini pope, Urban VIII (1623–44),
commissioned the work that brought Pietro
fame throughout Europe – the frescoes for
the Palazzo Barberini, culminating in an

*Allegory of Divine Providence and Barberini
Power* (1633–9) for the principal ceiling.
Urban VIII also commissioned the easel
painting *Reconciliation of Jacob and Laban*
(Louvre, Paris), to which the present
painting is closely related.

Faith, Hope and Charity constitutes a
reworking of the principal figures in the left
half of the *Reconciliation*. In the latter there
are two adult female figures and three
children, balancing the group of Jacob and
his wily uncle Laban shaking hands, with a
third male figure gathering up a bundle of
broken sticks (an emblem of discord, as well
as an allusion to the sticks used by Jacob in
his manipulation of the fertility of Laban's
flocks), on the right. The left-hand group in
the *Reconciliation* represents the two wives of
Jacob – Leah and Rachel – with some of

their numerous offspring. For *Faith, Hope
and Charity*,
the artist has elevated the leading female
(the fertile Leah) into a personification of
Charity, accompanied by Hope gazing into
the distance, while a new figure, Faith,
clutching her anchor, closes the composition
on the right. The sons of Jacob become
putti, one of whom is restrained from
offering an apple (suggestive, in classical and
Christian mythology, of discord) to the child
at Charity's breast. Charity herself, a figure
reminiscent of the Madonna in other
compositions by Pietro, confirms the
ambivalently Classical and Christian ethos
of the painting, and of the Roman
aristocracy at this period.   J.M.

Gambier-Parry Collection [P.1966.GP.316]

RUBENS, SIR PETER PAUL
1577–1640
Triptych:
(Centre) *The Descent from the Cross* 1611
(Left) *The Visitation* and (right) *The
Presentation in the Temple* 1613
Oil on panel: (centre) 115.2 x 76.2;
(side panels) 83.2 x 30.3 and 83 x 30.4

The oil sketch of *The Descent from the Cross*
is a preparatory study for the central panel
of the High Altarpiece in Antwerp
Cathedral, delivered there in 1612. The high
finish of this work indicates that it was
probably the contract version, that is, the
preliminary painting presented by Rubens
for approval by the Guild of Harquebusiers
(gunsmiths), which formally commissioned
the final Altarpiece on 7 September 1611.

The patron saint of the Guild of
Harquebusiers was St Christopher, who
had carried the Christ Child across the river;
and the overall theme of this panel and of
its side panels depicting *The Visitation* and
The Presentation in the Temple is the bearing
of Christ and the Salvation. The sketches
for the reverse of the wings, depicting
St Christopher and the Hermit respectively,
are in the Alte Pinakothek, Munich.

The theme of *The Descent from the Cross*
had been confronted by Rubens c.1600
in a free drawing (now in the Hermitage,
Leningrad) after a famous fresco of 1541 by
Daniele da Volterra in the church of Santa
Trinità dei Monti, Rome; Rubens was in
Rome from 1600 to 1608. As in the
Leningrad drawing, Rubens here includes,
at the upper right, the distinctive figure

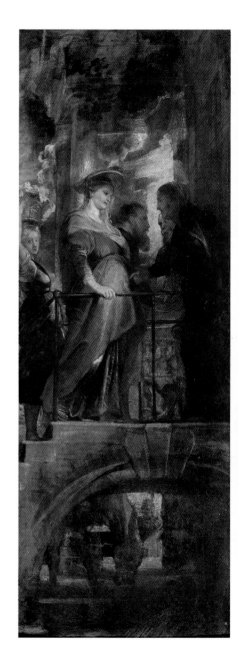

of the man clenching the shroud in his
teeth, and, with his back turned to the
spectator, the figure of St John the
Evangelist. Joseph of Arimathaea balances
on the ladder at the left. Grouped in the
foreground below him, and ready to
receive the legs and torso of Christ, are
the figures of the three Marys – the
Virgin, Mary Cleophas and Mary
Magdalen. For the curving, tortured
figure of Jesus, Rubens referred to a source
older than the Volterra fresco: the
Laocoön group (first century BC) in the
Vatican Collections. This celebrated
marble sculpture, with its writhing,
contorted male figures, was thought in
late sixteenth-century Rome to constitute
the ultimate expression of man's greatest
misery and suffering.

Less highly finished and coloured,
more loosely painted and smaller in scale,
are the sketches for *The Visitation* and
The Presentation in the Temple. These
works, completed in 1613, were probably
not presented for inspection before the
Harquebusiers Guild, but would have
been retained in Rubens's studio and
used for reference by both master and
pupils during the completion of the final
compositions. The finished wings were
delivered to Antwerp Cathedral only in
February and March 1614.

For this altarpiece, Rubens was paid the
substantial sum of 2,400 guilders.   W.B.

(Centre) Lee Collection [P.1947.LF.359];
(side panels) Princes Gate Collection
[P.1978.PG.361 and P.1978.PG.360]

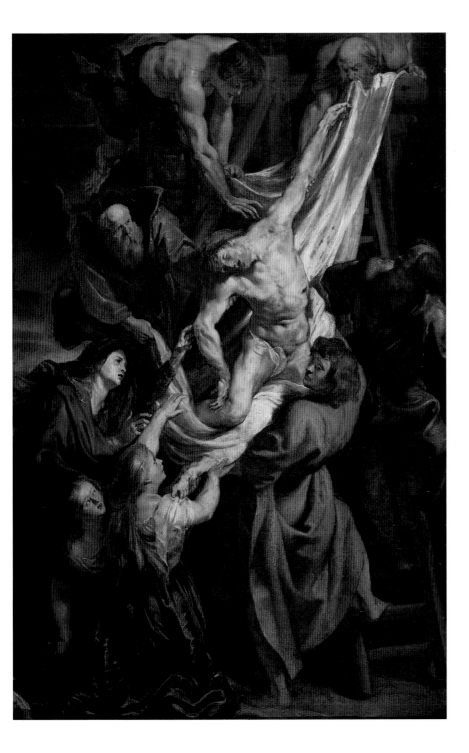

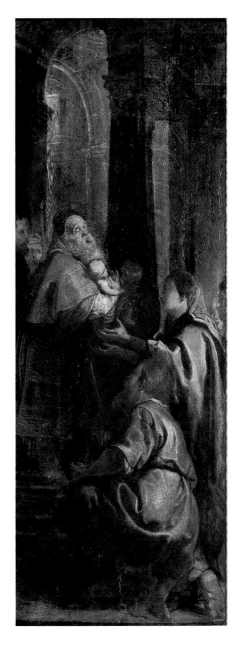

RUBENS, SIR PETER PAUL
1577–1640
The Family of Jan Bruegel the Elder c.1613–15
Oil on panel, 124.5 x 94.6

The Antwerp painter Jan Bruegel (1568–1625) is portrayed here with his wife Catharina van Marienberg and their two eldest children, Peter (b.1608) and Elisabeth (b.1609). A son of the famous Pieter Bruegel the Elder, Jan specialized in detailed cabinet paintings. He was a close friend of Rubens, with whom he collaborated on many works, and who acted as his secretary in his correspondence with his Italian patron, Cardinal Borromeo.

The portrait, painted c.1613–15, is remarkable for its intimacy and informality. With three pairs of eyes looking out of the picture, the viewer's attention is directly engaged by the sitters. Catharina's central position in the composition, which is analogous to that of the Virgin in a painting of the Holy Family, expresses her central role in the family as wife and mother. The impression of a close-knit family unit is conveyed largely through the interplay of arms and hands, particularly in their convergence on Catharina's lap. While Elisabeth gazes lovingly up at her mother, whose example, it is implied, she will aspire to follow, Peter's hand directs attention to her bracelet (one of a pair), probably a betrothal gift. Rubens's own wife Isabella Brant is depicted wearing a similar pair in their marriage portrait of 1609 (Munich, Alte Pinakothek).

No trappings of Jan Bruegel's profession appear here. The couple are portrayed as respectable Antwerp burghers, their restrained but rich dress contrasting with the fashionable clothes sported by their children, Peter amusingly adopting a courtier's pose. Elisabeth's expensive coral necklace is of a type that was believed to protect children against evil.

While it is possible that the figure of Jan Bruegel was introduced only at a late stage in the evolution of the picture (there is an early copy in which this figure is absent), there is little doubt that it was always intended that he should be included somewhere in the project, perhaps in the more traditional form of a pendant portrait. Rubens certainly integrated him convincingly into the spirit of the present composition. An allusion to the idea of conjugal and family love as the source of an artist's inspiration (a theme discernible in contemporary Northern Netherlandish portraiture) may have been intended here. The contrast between the tighter execution and blander lighting of Catharina and the livelier treatment of Jan is explicable as a visual means of differentiating their characters, a concern also evinced by the choice of a different type of ruff for each member of the family.

The fact that this painting, in which one leading Antwerp artist is portrayed by another, passed by marriage into the possession of a third (David Teniers II) vividly reflects the close ties that existed between members of the artistic community in the city. J.W./A.W.-L.

Princes Gate Collection [P.1978.PG.362]

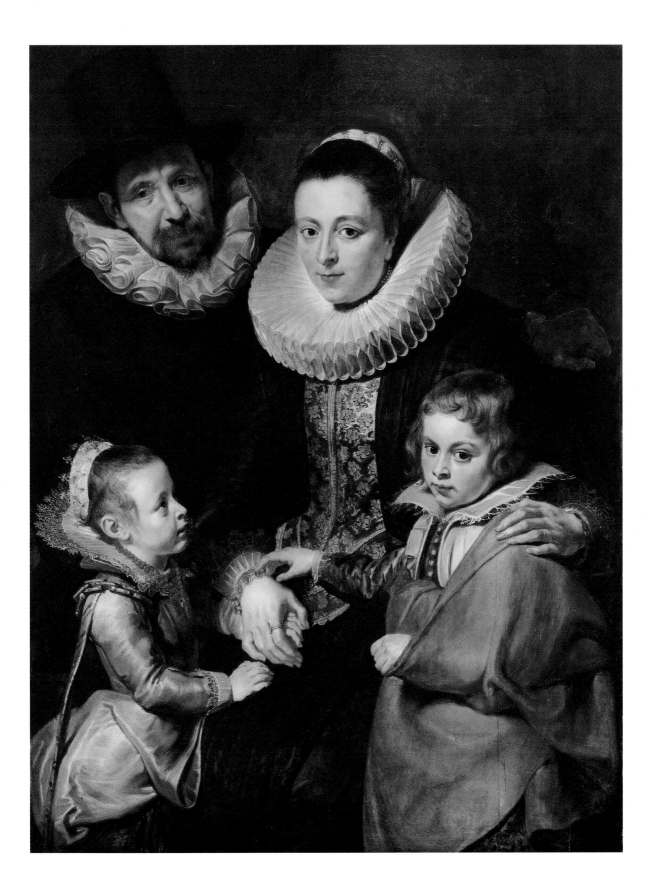

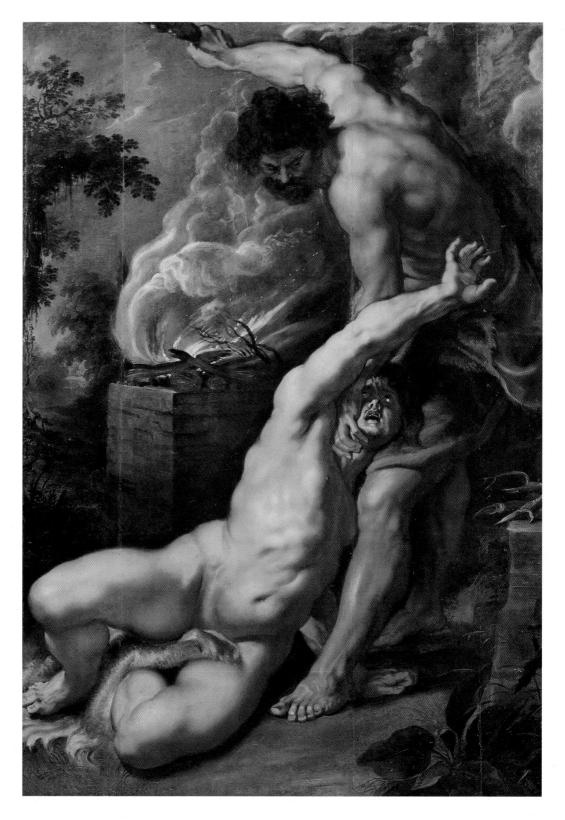

RUBENS, SIR PETER PAUL
1577–1640
Cain slaying Abel c.1608–9
Oil on panel, 131.2 x 94.2

This painting, dating from the time of Rubens's return to Antwerp from Italy and executed shortly before the closely

comparable *Moses and the Brazen Serpent* (also in the Princes Gate Collection), illustrates the interests and influences of the period. A number of Italian sixteenth-century sources have been proposed for the two figures – Michelangelo, Bandinelli, the Venetians – and the glimpse of landscape on the left is reminiscent of Elsheimer.

There is a copy of this painting at Blois, and an engraving (not in reverse) by Willem Buytewech of c.1612–13 also exists. A drawing by Rubens in Amsterdam (Amsterdams Historisch Museum) may be related.

Princes Gate Collection (1981) [P.1978.PG.353]

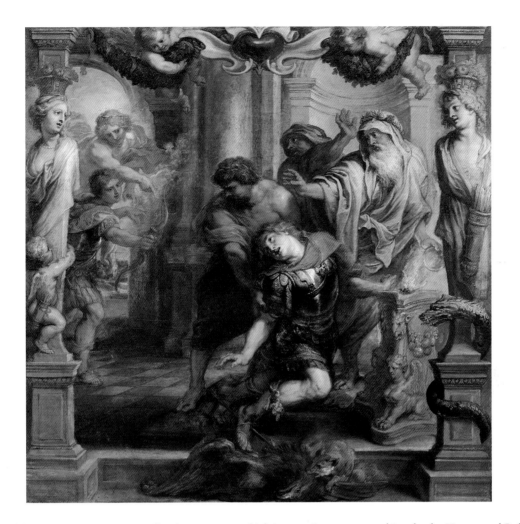

RUBENS, SIR PETER PAUL
1577–1640
The Death of Achilles early 1630s
Oil on panel, 107 x 108

The Death of Achilles is the final episode in a series of eight scenes from the life of the Greek hero, which served as designs for a cycle of tapestries. In the temple of Apollo at Thymbra, near Troy, where he is about to marry the princess Polyxena, Achilles falls victim to Trojan treachery. Guided by Apollo, the champion of the Trojan cause, Paris's arrow pierces Achilles' heel, his one vulnerable spot. The figure in lilac robes is probably the priest Calchas. Below the 'stage' on which the main drama takes place, a symbolic group echoes the central action: the mighty hero (eagle) is vanquished by the wily Paris (fox). Flanking the design are two sculpted herms of Venus (with Cupid) and Apollo (with the snake-like monster Python). In an amusing conceit, these deities appear to observe dispassionately the tragedy for which they between them were ultimately responsible. Above, a cartouche flanked by putti and swags completes the framing structure, which is a consistent, unifying feature of the eight scenes (cf. *The Wrath of Achilles* from the same series, also in the Princes Gate Collection).

Nothing definite is known about the origins of the project, but circumstantial evidence strongly suggests that the designs were produced in the early 1630s, perhaps as a speculative venture, for (or in collaboration with) Rubens's father-in-law, Daniel Fourment, an Antwerp tapestry dealer. The present *modello* is a faithful enlargement of an oil sketch (Rotterdam), and would have served both as the pattern for the full-scale cartoon from which the tapestry was woven, and as a contract painting, on the basis of which prospective clients might order a set of tapestries. Their high degree of finish would also have made such works saleable objects in their own right. Clarity of design and detail is typical of Rubens's *modelli* for projects like tapestries and engravings, the final execution of which was beyond his direct control.

The basic literary source of the life of Achilles is Homer's great epic, the *Iliad*. However, the demise of the hero is only hinted at by Homer, and Rubens drew here (as he did extensively in this series) on later, elaborated versions of the story. But while Renaissance commentators had interpreted the downfall of Achilles in moralistic terms, as a consequence of his 'lustful love' for Polyxena, Rubens rather stresses the drama and pathos of the event. Indeed, the expression and pose of the dying Achilles evoke the famous Classical sculptures of Laocoön (Vatican) and the Dying Alexander (Florence, Uffizi), which in Rubens's time were regarded as the supreme embodiment of pathos. Moreover, Laocoön had been a priest of the very temple of Apollo where the present scene takes place. The introduction of these associations is characteristic of Rubens's harnessing of the Antique to enrich his own art.

There was no precedent for such a comprehensive treatment of the life of Achilles, and Rubens, with his profound knowledge of Antiquity, must surely have relished the opportunity to display his erudition and powers of invention.   A.W.-L.

Princes Gate Collection [P.1978.PG.375]

51

RUBENS, SIR PETER PAUL
1577–1640
Landscape by Moonlight c.1637–8
Oil on panel, 64 x 90 cm

Rubens's landscape paintings have always been held in especial esteem in Britain. By the end of the eighteenth century most of them were already in British collections, and the *Landscape by Moonlight* certainly belonged to Sir Joshua Reynolds by 1778, when he displayed it at the Royal Academy to illustrate his Eighth Discourse. Since then, it has been among those well-known and admired works by Rubens that profoundly influenced the English school of landscape artists including, notably, Gainsborough and Constable, and was praised by critics ranging from Reynolds to Roger Fry. Whereas much of Rubens's work was commissioned, his landscapes stand apart as having been painted, it seems, purely for personal pleasure. A few were to pass to friends and favoured patrons, but many remained in his possession until his death.

Among these, *Landscape by Moonlight* hung either in his Antwerp town-house or at his country manor house, Het Steen, which

he acquired in 1635. During the last years of his life Rubens retired whenever possible to Het Steen with his young second wife, Helena Fourment, and increasing family. It was at that time that the present work and many of his greatest landscapes were painted, in private celebration of the peace and fecundity of the Brabant countryside.

The night setting seen here is exceptional, a return to the subject of 'night-pieces' first seen in what may have been Rubens's first landscape, of around 1613, an inspired version of a *Flight into Egypt* by Elsheimer, the German artist whom Rubens had known and admired in Rome and whose rare paintings he collected. Earth, trees and water are bathed in bright moonlight, the clouds pierced by brilliant stars, represented by dabs of pigment, one a shooting star; the moon and distant trees are repeated in reflections. Only the grazing horse inhabits this landscape and only the barn to the left implies a human presence.

Rubens achieved this effect of nocturnal solitude only after complex experiment. At first the panel was smaller, formed by two horizontal oak planks roughly three-quarters as high and two-thirds as wide: the joins of the additions to top and right are visible. At

different stages he experimented with various figures: a group including a mother and child, perhaps the Holy Family, seated around a fire beneath the largest tree; a band of indistinct figures sketched in roughly to the right, after enlargement of the panel; at some point a lantern hung also to the right, while the horse was evidently added at some intermediate stage.

Examination using X-radiographs and infra-red reflectography and analysis of layers of paint samples have revealed this much, but raise new questions about the figure subjects, their degree of finish and sequence in this process. Bolswert's contemporary engraving demonstrates that Rubens himself painted out the figures. Clear to the eye are his changes in the position and outline of trees and the intense diversity in technique between the highly finished smaller panel and the freely handled additions.

The artist deceives us about this evolutionary process, presenting for our contemplation an intensely personal vision. Here, with poetic imagination, Rubens heralds the landscapists whom he was later to inspire. H.B.

Princes Gate Collection [P.1978.PG.380]

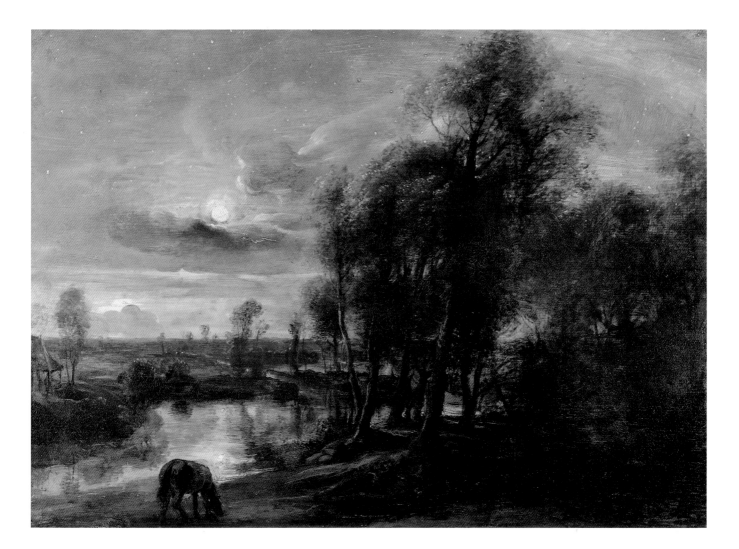

CLAUDE GELLÉE (called Claude
Lorrain) 1600–82
Landscape with an Imaginary View of Tivoli
1642
Oil on copper, 21.6 x 25.8
Signed and dated, lower left: 'CLAVDIO[?]
1642'

This little painting is dated 1642, but the
circumstances of its origin are not known.
Claude made no reference to a patron or
to a destination in his record of the work
(no. 67) in the *Liber Veritatis*; and the
addition by a later hand of the name
'Robert Gayer', who was not born until
c.1639, is misleading (this is thought to
refer to Gayer's probable possession of a
variant of the picture, which is now at
Petworth and is almost certainly not by
Claude). It seems likely that the present
painting was executed as a memento for
a traveller on his departure from Rome.

The date places the work at the end of
Claude's earlier period when, in common
with his painter friends from northern
Europe, he had produced genre scenes: busy
seaports which had occupied his imagination
since an earlier stay in Naples, or landscapes
with groups of musicians or dancers, or a
herdsman with his cattle and goats. By the
later 1640s there began to evolve what we
think of as typical Claudian work: classical,
biblical, or pastoral subjects quietly absorbed
into the idyllic landscape of the Roman
Campagna, where the light seems almost
timeless, yet is appropriate to the hour. In a
distinction made by the late Anthony Blunt,
what had been viewed with curiosity by
earlier artists was now seen by Claude with
the eyes of wonder.

In 1642, however, that trend was
foreshadowed only in hints, and this
painting is less sophisticated. The
foreground is busy with its herdsman and
his animals, and with the abundant plant life
which would have delighted Elsheimer.
Across a wooden bridge moves a horseman
with his party – one of Claude's last figures
depicted in contemporary dress, soon to be
succeeded by characters from mythology or
the scriptures. Beyond the bridge the river is
agitated by the falls, sheltered on the left by
great trees, and overlooked on the right by
the temple of the Sybil, as well as by the villa
of Maecenas, only just visible, and a
Romanesque church tower – a cluster of
buildings doing poetic duty for Tivoli itself.
The river winds towards the horizon where
the dome of St Peter's seen in silhouette
reminds us, as it would have reminded
Claude's patron, of the not-so-distant
Eternal City. Meanwhile, the light of the
early evening sun edges the clouds and the
woodwork of the bridge with bright touches
of gold, reserving for the distance a more
subdued, serener light.

This work is painted on copper – a
support which Claude used on fifteen or
more occasions, but which gradually lost
its popularity during his lifetime.   R.H.

Princes Gate Collection [P.1978.PG.64]

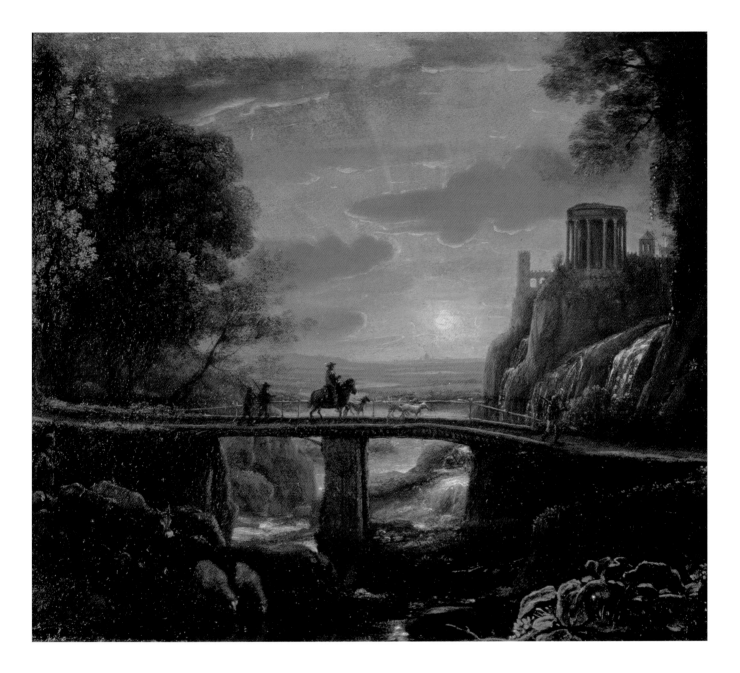

VAN DYCK, ANTHONY 1599–1641
The Adoration of the Shepherds c.1616–18
Oil on canvas, 115.3 x 163.7

In an English context, Anthony van Dyck is famous as the greatest portrait painter of the seventeenth century, an artist who provided the English aristocracy with the image of itself that it most wished were true, and who continued as the strongest single influence on high-style British portraiture from William Dobson in the 1640s (see pp. 58–9) to Sargent and de Laszlo in the early twentieth century.

Van Dyck began his active career in Antwerp, the principal city of the Spanish Netherlands and the northern citadel of Catholic power. His earliest works show his understanding of the place assigned to art by Counter-Reformation theology as an aid to devotion, and in particular as an aid to the imaginative comprehension of the Gospels and the lives of the saints as real events affecting real people. While still in his mid-teens, his precocious brilliance gained him a place in Rubens's busy studio, where c.1615 he almost certainly worked on the large

altarpiece of the *Adoration of the Shepherds,* now in the Musée des Beaux-Arts, Rouen. In the latter, the Virgin, accompanied by St Joseph, appears bathed in a shaft of light from on high in which angelic *putti* dance. Three male shepherds and three females stoop in adoration towards the Child, who is suckling; in the foreground, one of the shepherdesses adds a fourth egg to the three already lying on hay beside the Child. Apart from the *putti* and the divine light, the scene is essentially naturalistic. The interior of the stable and the sturdy rural people have been recognizably borrowed from contemporary Flemish models.

That sense of naturalism, as well as the overall dynamics of the scene and many of the actual details of the Rubens altarpiece, recur in the present picture. In particular, the elderly female figure in the white headdress and the younger woman holding the egg are clearly the same, except that the latter is now shown offering the egg directly to the Child, rather than simply placing it with the others.

The whole tradition of the placing of the Nativity, and the subsequent adoration by

the wise men and the shepherds, in a stable occupied by animals depends from Apocryphal interpretations of the passage in Isaiah I, 3, 'The ox knoweth his owner, and the ass his master's crib: but Israel doth not know . . .', overlaying the basic Gospel story which mentions only a manger. From the earliest times, Christian visualizations of the scene frequently represented the stable as a ruined building, making it symbolic of the Old Dispensation, within which the New Dispensation of the Christian era is born. Here the young Van Dyck, following Rubens, reinforces the prophetic aspect of the scene with the detail of the egg, an unconventional addition to the traditional iconography of the Nativity. The latter, in popular culture a symbol of the tomb as well as of birth, predicts the crucifixion, burial and resurrection of Christ, and has increasingly supplanted candlesticks and candles in the celebration of Easter.

For another, earlier appearance of the egg as a gift by a shepherdess, see Tintoretto, *The Adoration of the Shepherds* (p. 42). J.M.

Princes Gate Collection [P.1978.PG.102]

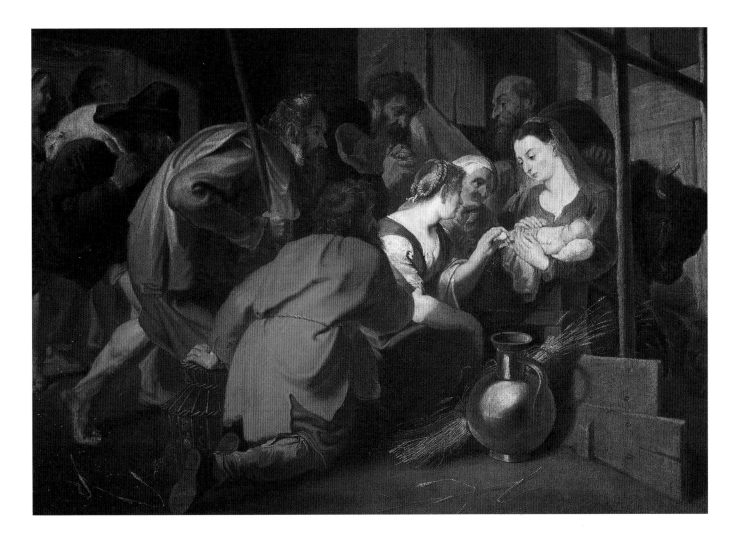

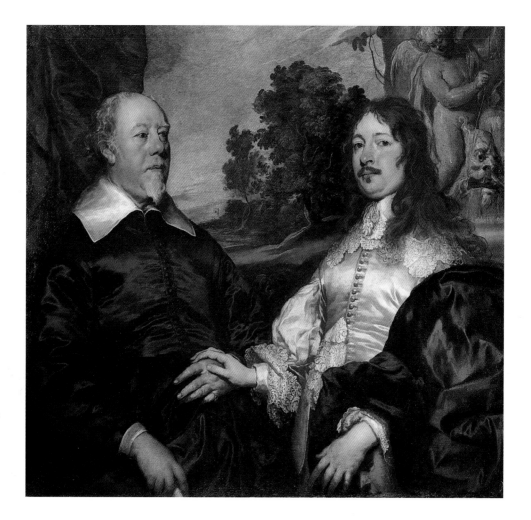

DOBSON, WILLIAM 1611–46
Portrait of an Old and a Younger Man
c.1641–2

Oil on canvas, 110.5 x 119 (including a strip
of canvas measuring 15.5 x 19.5 cm added on
the right-hand side by the artist).

The seventeenth-century pioneer of the art
of biography, John Aubrey, characterized
William Dobson as 'the most excellent
painter that England hath yet bred'.
Biographically, Aubrey was interested in
portraiture as providing a record of the
appearance of men and women whose lives
had been of historical significance. It was
fortunate that, following the death of Van
Dyck in December 1641, Dobson was at
hand to record the faces of the principal
actors in the great national drama that was
beginning to unfold.

Dobson's short career was largely limited
to the early 1640s, covering the departure of
King Charles I and his Court from London
in January 1642, and the return of defeated
loyalists to the capital in the summer of
1646. All his patrons were involved in the

war-fever and initial hopes occasioned by the
King's raising of his standard at Nottingham
in 1642, and were affected by his long series
of defeats that culminated in the Battle of
Naseby in 1645. They are mostly men; they
wear armour and officer's sashes, and their
expressions reflect the emotional upheavals
in families on both sides of the conflict.

The present painting belongs early in
Dobson's career, possibly even to the last
months of the pre-War period. There have
been many suggestions as to the identity of
the sitters, and the significance of the
touching hands. The two men have been
seen as any father and son caught up in
private grief, comforting one another,
possibly on the death of wife and mother.

But Dobson's ability to seize likeness and
to suggest emotion is combined here with a
pictorial structure that suggests dislocation
rather than engagement between the
individuals. So the two men have also been
seen as representing opposing tendencies in
Church and State, the old man as Puritan
and Parliamentarian, the young man as
Laudian and Royalist, at the sad parting
of their ways. At a less topical level of

interpretation, the reverie of the older man
suggests a philosophical withdrawal from the
world. The rural setting and black silk
costume suggest the Renaissance cult of
Melancholy, while the young man, brightly
dressed and in eye-contact with the
spectator, his arm resting on what may be a
head of Venus, in front of Cupid hooking
a sea-monster, seems to declare for the
primrose path.

The painting thus deals with familiar
themes of classicizing literature and art, the
contrast between youth and age, town and
country, the worldly and the philosophical,
the pleasures of the flesh and the refinement
of high ideas. Dobson's work almost always
has such an extra dimension of emblematic
significance beyond a solidly conceived
present. Brilliant and rapid in execution,
and as vivid in individual likeness as the
famous works of Titian, Van Dyck or
Rubens, Dobson's portraits seem to
elevate the individual sitter into a type,
and the passing moment into a realm of
timeless significance.   J.M.

Lee Collection [P.1947.LF.97]

58

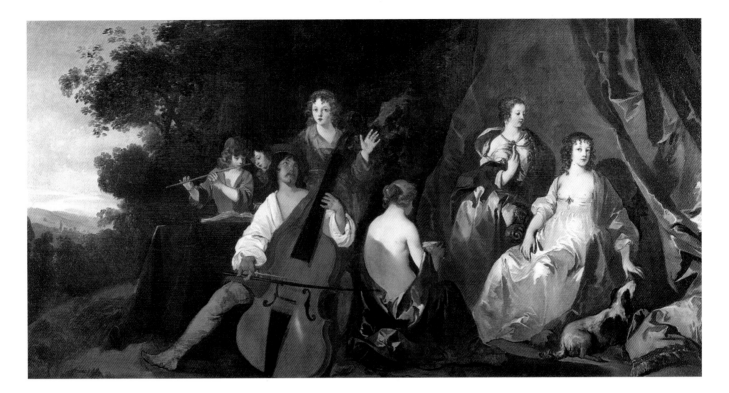

LELY, SIR PETER 1618–80
The Concert ('Lely and his Family')
late 1640s
Oil on canvas, 122.9 x 234.5

Sir Peter Lely, the son of a Dutch army
captain named van der Faes, was born at
Soest, Westphalia; he returned to Holland,
where he trained under Peter de Grebber
at Haarlem and became a Master in the
Haarlem Guild in 1637. The nickname by
which he became known was derived from
one of the houses, 'In de Lely', owned by his
family in The Hague. Nothing is known of
his work before he came to London, where
he most probably arrived in 1643. His first
certain portraits date from 1647, when he
began to be patronized by the Earl of
Northumberland, who introduced him
to other noblemen.

During the Commonwealth and
Protectorate, Lely painted mythological
and historical pieces, as well as portraits,
including one of Oliver Cromwell. He
amassed a large personal fortune during
the 1650s and began to collect Old Master
paintings and drawings on a considerable

scale, including works by Van Dyck sold
from Charles I's collection. The portraits of
this period are often austere in mood,
although he could achieve a more playfully
baroque style in portrait groups and 'fancy
conversation pieces', of which *The Concert*
is one. These belong either to the late 1640s
or, less likely, to 1658–9, after Lely's return to
London from a prolonged visit to Holland.
Although *The Concert* has been called 'An
Idyll', and, at least as early as 1763, 'Lely and
his Family', there is no foundation for this
traditional identification. The seated
musician depicted here may, however, be
a self-portrait.

Painted with a vibrant touch in clear, fresh
colours, this enchanting group shows seven
figures, including two young children and a
young woman gathered round the figure of
a casually dressed man who plays a bass-
violin (five-stringed cello). One child plays
a flute and his two companions sing from
a score to the accompaniment of the two
instrumentalists. The half-draped female
nude, also holding a sheet of music, with her
back half-turned to the bass-player, acts as
a pivotal figure in the composition, linking

the right-hand group of elegantly attired
women and their dogs with the musicians
on the left. A rich, plum-coloured expanse
of silken material hangs down on the right
like a theatrical backdrop, which half-
envelops the woman standing by her
companion who is seated on a throne.
On the left, beyond the rocky outcrop, we
catch a glimpse of a distant landscape and
ruins. It is as if we have surprised a discreetly
'bohemian' picnic party in some idealized
sylvan glade. The painting looks back in
colour and mood to the *fêtes champêtres* of
sixteenth-century Venetian art and
amusingly anticipates Manet's *Le Déjeuner
sur l'herbe* (see p. 71). The courtly flavour of
the Lely painting echoes the poetry of his
friend, the cavalier Richard Lovelace, and
reflects Lely's own love of music. Some of
the foreground drapery and other details
are unfinished.

The meaning of the picture is obscure,
but Oliver Millar has suggested that it
represents the familiar allegory of Music
in the service of Love and Beauty.   D.F.

Lee Collection [P.1947.LF.216]

59

TIEPOLO, GIOVANNI BATTISTA
1696–1770
Allegory of the Power of Eloquence c.1725
Oil on canvas, 46.5 x 67.5; within shaped border

This is a *modello* for Tiepolo's first surviving ceiling fresco decoration for the main *salone* on the second floor of the Palazzo Sandi in Venice, in the parish of S. Angelo, near the Grand Canal. The Sandi family had been ennobled in 1685, and were professionally associated with the law. The allegorical subject chosen for this painting may be an allusion to the Sandi family's legal distinction, but as Michael Levey points out in his monograph on the artist (1986), the triumph of mind over matter, of verbal cunning over brute force, has been extended to the power of sound, not only through words but through music. Minerva and Mercury occupy the centre of the stage as the deities of Wisdom and Eloquence.

The subsidiary themes occupying the four sides of the ceiling fresco (which may still be seen in the Palazzo Sandi) appear in this preliminary sketch, but they undergo some important changes in the final scheme as the artist tightens up the composition in order to link more closely the five constituent elements, as well as to heighten the overall dramatic effect. Painted on a red ground, the *modello* may lack the sparkle and luminosity seen in the final fresco, but it provides us with an interesting insight into Tiepolo's rapidly developing creative genius.

The four supporting heroic themes are, clockwise from the bottom: Amphion, by the power of music, causing the walls of Thebes to build themselves; Orpheus leading Eurydice past Cerberus; Hercules 'Gallicus' enchaining people by the power of speech; and Bellerophon on his winged horse, Pegasus, slaying the Chimera. The most important group is of Amphion surrounded by the amazed Thebans, and it was this scene which would be the first to confront the spectator as he entered the room and looked up at the ceiling. Tiepolo did, however, alter the positions of the Bellerophon and Orpheus groups (right and left, respectively, in the *modello*) on the finished ceiling, by placing Bellerophon on the left side and substituting Hercules in his place. Orpheus is moved to the top of the composition, thereby strengthening the link between the two 'musical' elements, and placing Bellerophon and Hercules in counterpoint. Tiepolo has also more satisfactorily integrated Minerva and Mercury into the final composition, by making them larger and creating around them two almost interlocking whirlpools of cloud, which, in turn, act as a foil to a brilliantly lit golden empyrean that has been only tentatively indicated in this preliminary *modello*.

The Palazzo Sandi frescoes were almost certainly finished by 1726, for in June of that year Tiepolo recevied a commission to paint decorations in a chapel of the Duomo in Udine.   D.F.

Princes Gate Collection [P.1978.PG.445]

60

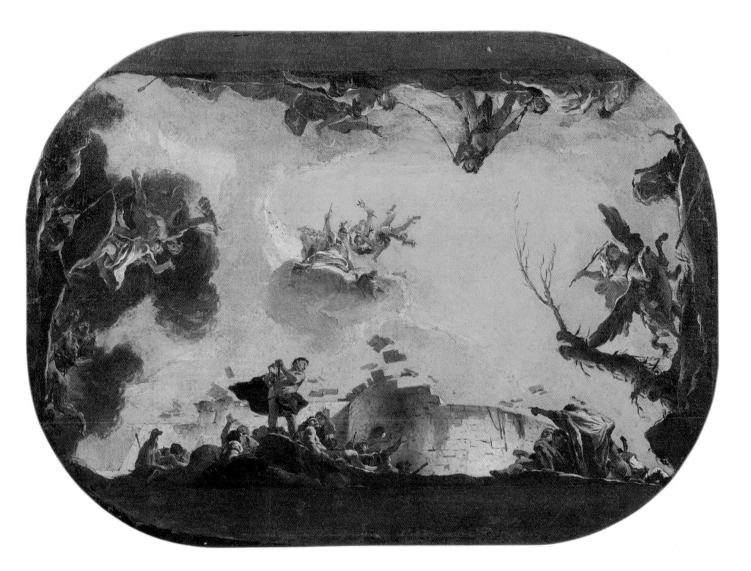

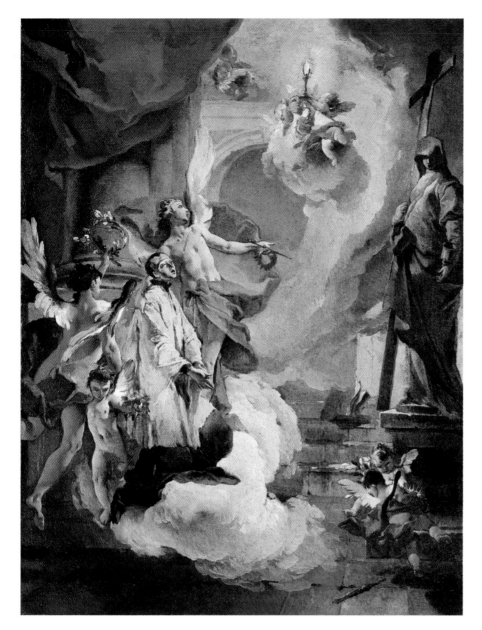

TIEPOLO, GIOVANNI BATTISTA
1696–1770
St Aloysius (Luigi) Gonzaga in Glory
c.1726(?)
Oil on canvas, 58.1 x 44.6
Contemporary inscription on verso:
'Gio: Batta: Tiepolo 1735'

Aloysius Gonzaga (1568–91), a Jesuit of
noble birth who died young, was canonized
in 1726; he is the patron saint of Catholic
youth. It has been suggested that the present
picture, which corresponds in style with

other works by Tiepolo of about the same
date, was painted on this occasion; it
appears to be a *modello* for an unexecuted
altarpiece. The inscription on the back
cannot refer to the date of execution, but
may record the gift of the painting to the
family of the sculptor Andrea Fantoni, who
had just made the frame for Tiepolo's
altarpiece for the parish church at Rovetta
(1734, installed 1736), and had died the
same year, 1734.

Princes Gate Collection (1981) [P.1978.PG.447]

Opposite:
*TIEPOLO AND THE MONASTERY
CHURCH OF S. PASCUAL (PASCHAL)
AT ARANJUEZ*

Giovanni Battista Tiepolo's last major
commission was for seven altarpieces in the
monastery church of the Discalced
(barefoot) Franciscans at Aranjuez, south of
Madrid, built under royal patronage by
Francesco Sabatini, 1765–70. All five of the
known surviving *modelli* for the project are
in the Princes Gate Collection; two of them
are illustrated here, *St Paschal Baylon's Vision
of the Eucharist* and *The Stigmatization of
St Francis*.

Tiepolo received this commission in 1767,
after five years at the court of Charles III of
Spain, whose delegate for the present
commission was the king's confessor Joaquin
de Eleta. Eleta's hostility, it appears, and
perhaps also the rivalry of the court painter
Anton Mengs and his followers caused
difficulties and delay, and eventually the
dispersal of the seven altarpieces and even
in some cases their mutilation. By 1769, and
with the aid of Tiepolo's son Domenico, the
paintings were completed – subject to
approval – but were not installed in the
church until after the artist's death in the
following year.

Antonio Ponz's *Viage de España* (1772)
describes Tiepolo's altarpieces in the church,
with the exception of *St Charles Borromeo*,
for which a Crucifix had been substituted.
Within a few years Tiepolo's work was
replaced by that of Mengs, Bayeu and
Maella, which survived apparently until the
Civil War. The disposition of Tiepolo's
altarpieces can be reconstructed with the
aid of Ponz's account: those represented by
the present *modelli* were for the high altar
(*St Paschal Baylon's Vision of the Eucharist*),
and the east wall of the south transept
(*The Stigmatization of St Francis*). Where
the upper part of an altarpiece survives, its
original shape can be traced, corresponding
with the shape of its *modello*, and with its
frame, still in the church.

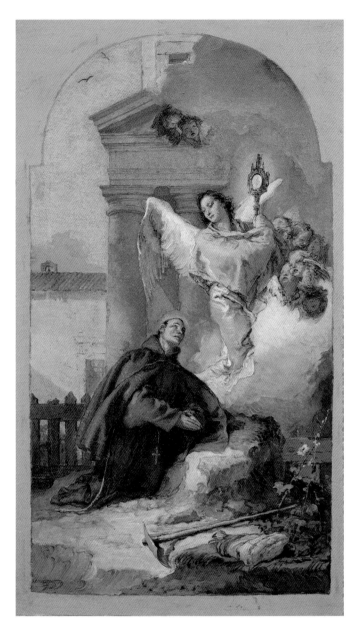
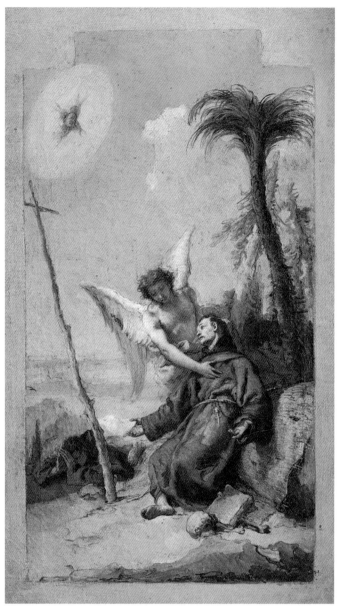

TIEPOLO, GIOVANNI BATTISTA
1696–1770

St Paschal Baylon's Vision of the Eucharist
1767
Oil on canvas, 63.6 x 38.7, within shaped
border; internal measurements 58 x 32.3

Modello for the high altar of the monastery
church. Two large fragments of the
altarpiece survive in the Prado, Madrid,
and the whole is recorded in an etching
by Domenico Tiepolo, whose inscription
indicates that it was his father's last work,
finally completed in 1770. A drawing by
G.B. Tiepolo of the angel holding the
monstrance, also in the Princes Gate

Collection, must post-date the *modello.*
It shows the only significant change
introduced in the finished work: the angel
no longer holds the monstrance with the
humeral veil prescribed for the priestly ritual
of Mass. This change was perhaps requested
by Padre Eleta after the initial completion of
the altarpiece in 1769. St Paschal, to whom
the church is dedicated, was a sixteenth-
century Spanish Discalced Franciscan,
whose occupation as gardener is alluded to
in the painting; he was noted for his
devotion to the cult of the Sacrament and
saw in a vision angels presenting the
Eucharist in a monstrance.

Princes Gate Collection (1981) [P.1978.PG.454]

The Stigmatization of St Francis 1767
Oil on canvas, 63.5 x 38.9, within shaped
border; internal measurements 55.5 x 30.5

Modello for the altarpiece formerly in the
south transept of S. Pascual, and now in the
Prado, intact, and signed 'Dn Juan Tiepolo
inv. et pinx.' The changes incorporated in
the finished painting include the elimination
of the Cross and the praying Franciscan,
Brother Leo, seen here on the left, and a
more conventional upward gaze of the saint.
Faint indications in the *modello* suggest
that this work may initially have been
round-headed.

Princes Gate Collection (1981) [P.1978.PG.455]

63

ROMNEY, GEORGE 1734–1802
Portrait of Georgiana, Lady Greville
c.1771–2
Oil on canvas, 76.2 x 63.5

Georgiana Peachey (1752–72) married
George, Lord Greville, on 1 April 1771, and it
seems that this portrait was painted around
the time of her marriage. Lord Greville later
became the second Earl of Warwick, but his
wife, having died on their first wedding
anniversary, in 1772, never became Countess
of Warwick. On marrying Lord Greville,
however, she joined a family who had
patronized some of the leading British
portrait painters of the day: George Greville
had been painted at the age of eight by
Sir Joshua Reynolds, who was to become
President of the Royal Academy in London;
that painting still hangs at Warwick Castle,
the family seat, where Greville was born.
Both Reynolds and Romney were also to
paint Greville's second wife, Henrietta
Vernon, whom he married four years after

the death of Georgiana, and Romney also
painted Henrietta's sister, Catherine Vernon,
in the character of 'Hebe'.

Such representations of aristocratic sitters
'in character' allowed portrait painters like
Reynolds and Romney to compliment the
moral qualities of their sitters through
comparison with literary or historical
characters, as well as raising the status of
'face painting' to something that began to
approach the demands made, on both
painter and viewer, by history painting.
For this portrait, however, the sitter is not
shown in character, but stands against a
hazily suggested sky, a translucent chemisette
crossed over her neck, and her body covered
by a lace-edged black cloak. With her gloved
hands folded before her, Lady Greville
modestly looks away to the right, rather than
meeting the gaze of the viewer head on, as
befitted a young woman (she would have
been about twenty) of her social status; it
would have offended contemporary notions
of propriety for her to gaze directly into the

eyes of either the male painter or the male
viewers of the portrait.

Like his fellow portrait painters, Reynolds
and Gainsborough, Romney felt the
limitations of the mere 'face painting'
demanded by the upper sectors of
eighteenth-century British society; over five
thousand drawings by Romney survive (the
largest single group is in the Fitzwilliam
Museum, Cambridge), bearing witness to
the range of his interests in subjects from
literature ranging from Greek drama to
Shakespeare and the Bible, as well as
allegorical subjects and aspects of
contemporary history. Indeed, Romney's
ambitions to become more than a mere
portrait painter led him, soon after painting
this portrait, to move to Italy in order to
study the collections of paintings and
sculpture which would give him the
knowledge and experience considered vital
for the production of history painting. S.H.

Lee Collection [P.1947.LF.344]

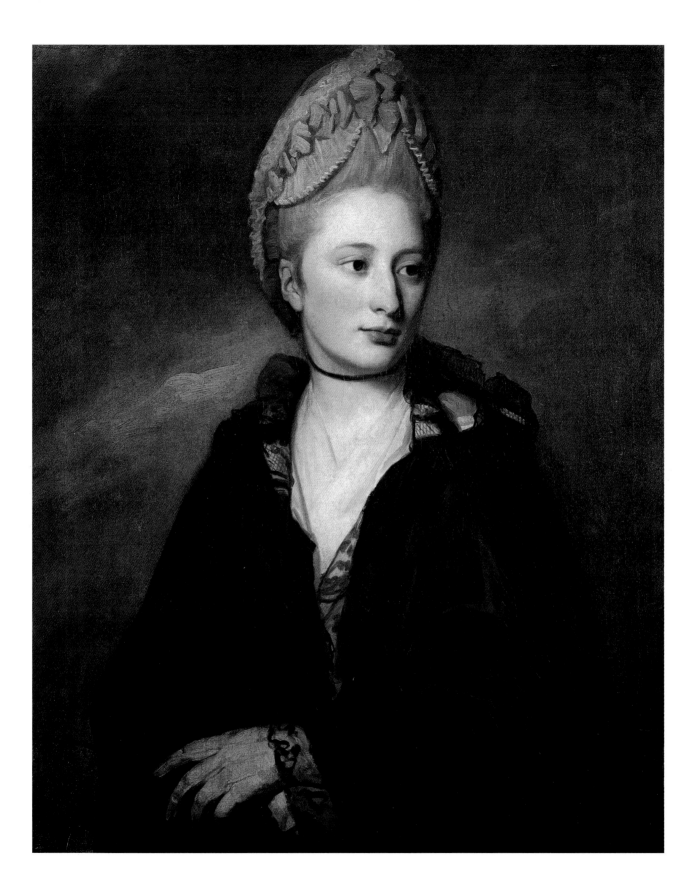

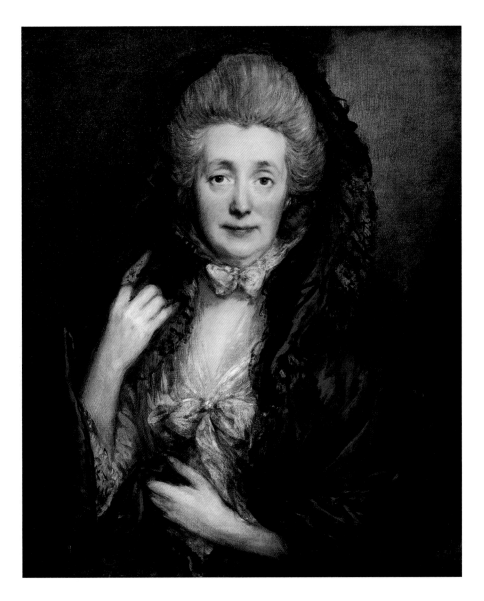

GAINSBOROUGH, THOMAS
1727–88
Portrait of Mrs Gainsborough c.1778–9
Oil on canvas, 76.6 x 63.8

Margaret Burr (born in 1728) married Thomas Gainsborough in 1746, when she was only eighteen and he a year older, and it has been suggested that this portrait was painted to celebrate her fiftieth birthday. Since their marriage Gainsborough had become one of the leading portrait painters in England. Tradition in Margaret Gainsborough's family has it that Gainsborough painted a portrait of his wife every year on their wedding anniversary, though few portraits of her survive.

This portrait is striking for its suggestion of intimacy between painter and sitter; Mrs Gainsborough is shown with her body and face pointing straight towards the viewer, her eyes meeting our gaze directly, her lips

slightly curved into what may be a smile, but which also suggests resignation. Equally striking is the mantle edged with black lace which she wears draped over her head and shoulders; this is formed from a powerful swirl of energetic brush-strokes around her head, which, continued by the position of her hands, suggests a subtle, personalized version of the painted architectural ovals within which many more formal eighteenth-century portraits were framed.

Towards the later part of his career, Gainsborough's handling of paint became increasingly rhythmic and flowing. Working with thinned paints, he experimented with ever bolder effects of transparency and light. In fact, it may be possible to see in the strong back-lighting illuminating the sitter's left side – throwing the delicately patterned black lace into silhouette – a reflection of Gainsborough's experiments with the newly fashionable art of painting transparent

images on glass. Such images, when lit from behind by flickering candlelight, could produce a startling effect of glowing and moving light. During the mid-1770s Gainsborough painted a number of landscape images on glass to be viewed through a magnifying lens in a specially constructed 'peep-show' box (now in the Victoria and Albert Museum), and it is possible that his interest in such lighting effects spilled over into his portraiture.

This portrait was one of the first paintings to be acquired by Samuel Courtauld, who bought it in 1921, along with a work he believed to be a self-portrait by Thomas Gainsborough painted as a pendant to this portrait of his wife; the portrait of the artist is now thought to be either a copy, or at least to have been completed, by his nephew and studio assistant, Gainsborough Dupont. S.H.

Courtauld Collection [P.1932.SC.157]

66

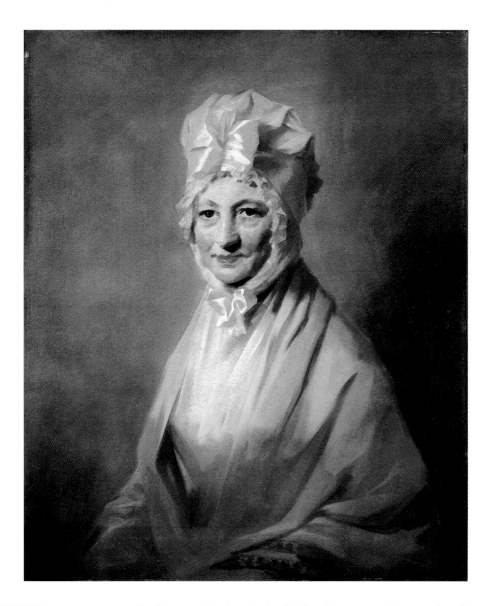

RAEBURN, SIR HENRY 1756–1823
Portrait of Mrs Malcolm c.1798–1802
Oil on canvas, 75.9 x 63.5

Unlike many of his compatriots, Raeburn resisted the lure of the English capital and spent most of his working life in his native Edinburgh. His output of portraits was enormous: he produced around a thousand paintings, the vast majority of which showed Scottish men and women of the landed, professional and trading classes, during a period of Scottish history when Edinburgh was frequently referred to as the 'Athens of the North'. By the early nineteenth century, Raeburn had established himself as the leading portrait painter in Scotland, and towards the end of his life his success was recognized by his admission as a member of the Royal Academy in London and of the Edinburgh Royal Society; he was knighted in 1822.

The sitter for this portrait, Margaret Pasley (a variant spelling of the name now more commonly spelled 'Paisley') was born in 1742 in Dumfriesshire, and, around 1761, she married George Malcolm, who farmed a neighbouring property. Their seventeen children included eleven sons, four of whom became knights; Margaret Malcolm is known now as the mother of the famous 'Four Knights of Dumfries'. The Courtauld painting may have been commissioned as a pendant to Raeburn's portrait of George Malcolm (Scottish National Portrait Gallery, Edinburgh, on loan from a private collector); there are in existence at least two sets of copies of the pair of portraits.

Mrs Malcolm is shown wearing a mob cap tied under her chin, a white kerchief over her chest, and a shawl with a narrow patterned border around her shoulders. Small in build, she is modestly dressed and posed in a manner then considered appropriate for a respectable woman in her late fifties or early sixties. S.H.

Lee Collection [P.1947.LF.334]

GOYA, FRANCISCO DE 1746–1828
Portrait of Don Francisco de Saavedra 1798
Oil on canvas, 200.2 x 119.6
Signed, on side of table: 'Savedra por Goya'

Don Francisco de Saavedra was a liberal who was appointed Minister of Finance to Carlos IV of Spain in November 1797; his fellow liberal, Gaspar Melchior de Jovellanos, was created Minister of Justice in the spring of 1798. In March 1798, Saavedra succeeded Godoy as Secretary of State. Both he and Jovellanos were bitterly opposed to Godoy, and both began to disappear from public life in August 1798; Saavedra was formally dismissed in February 1799.

The portrait of Saavedra is the later companion-piece to the portrait of Jovellanos (Prado, Madrid). The latter portrait was painted in the spring of 1798, and Jovellanos – a friend and admirer of Goya's for some time before the portrait was painted – paid the artist 6,000 *reales*

for it. While engaged on this work, Goya was asked to make a likeness of Saavedra. Although the painter was unable to comply immediately with this request, it is probable that the portrait commemorating Saavedra's Ministry was painted shortly after that of Jovellanos.

In both paintings the subject faces right, seated against a dark background on a round-backed chair – apparently the same in both canvases – with a table occupying the lower right area of the composition. Whereas Jovellanos, in pensive mood, is shown resting his elbow on the table, hand supporting his cheek, Saavedra is depicted in a more formally upright posture, although the rather clumsy, casual pose of his legs might indicate a certain unconventional side to his character.

In comparison with the richly decorated furniture, the statue of Minerva and the indications of background drapery in the portrait of Jovellanos, the present work seems simple, almost sparse. Here, the

background is broken only by rectilinear divisions – wall-panels, perhaps, and the suggestion of the frame of a mirror or picture. The simplicity of the design is almost certainly influenced by an acquaintanceship with English eighteenth-century portraiture, first evident in Goya's work dating from some twenty years earlier. However, it is clear that many of the more delicately brushed paint glazes, and perhaps some thicker applications of paint, had been removed before the picture entered the Courtauld collections; this now stark image would have been relieved by the virtuoso handling of paint visible in Jovellanos's portrait. Chief among the losses are the tassles at the hem of the tablecloth (only two of which remain entire, though ghostly images of others are visible) and the modelling of the (velvet?) breeches. There is also a considerable area of repainting to the right of the sitter's left shoulder.   W.B.

Lee Collection [P.1947.LF.180]

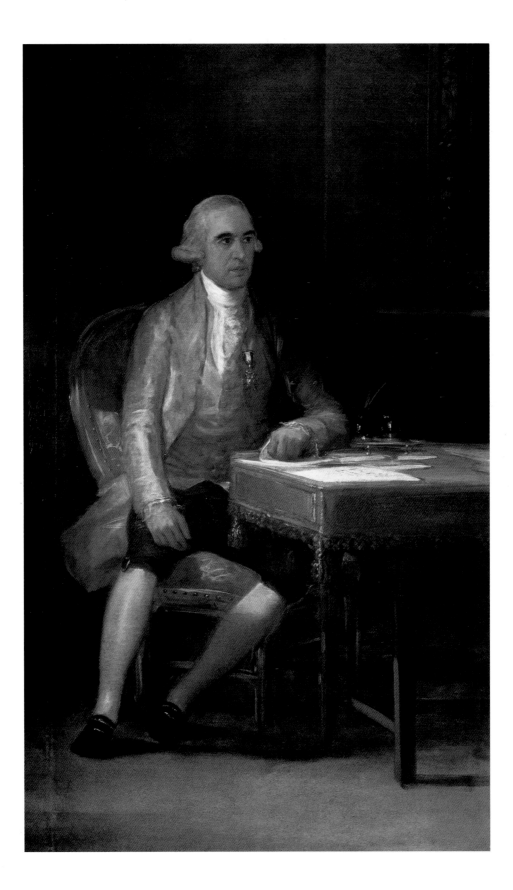

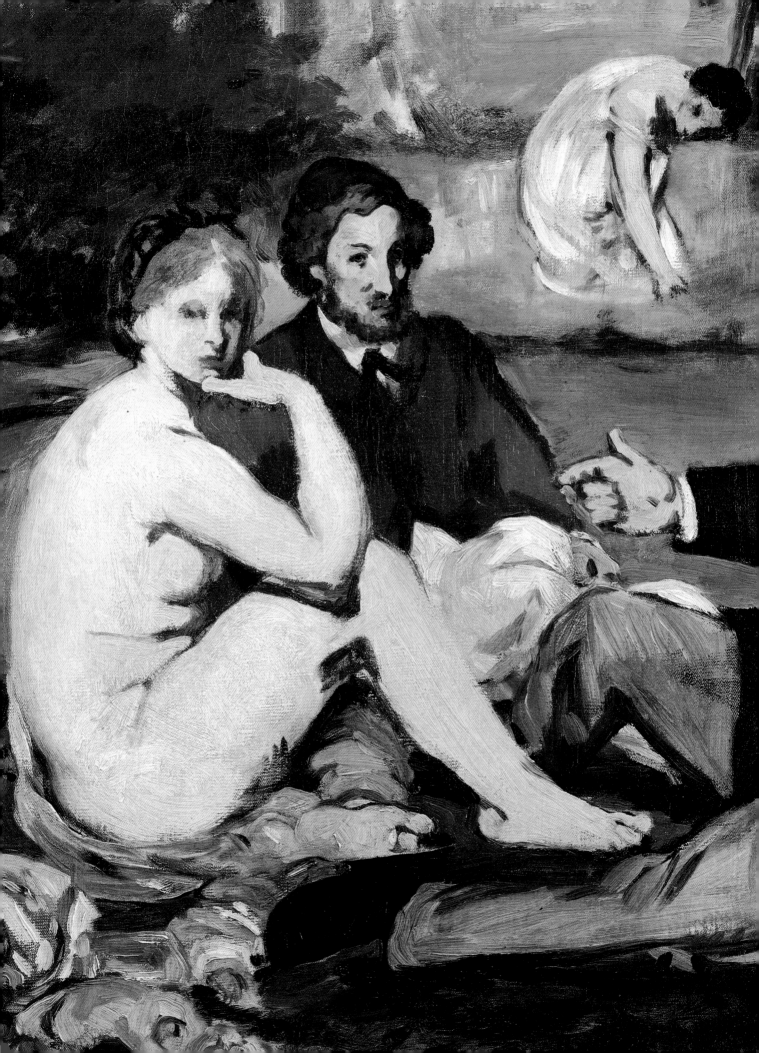

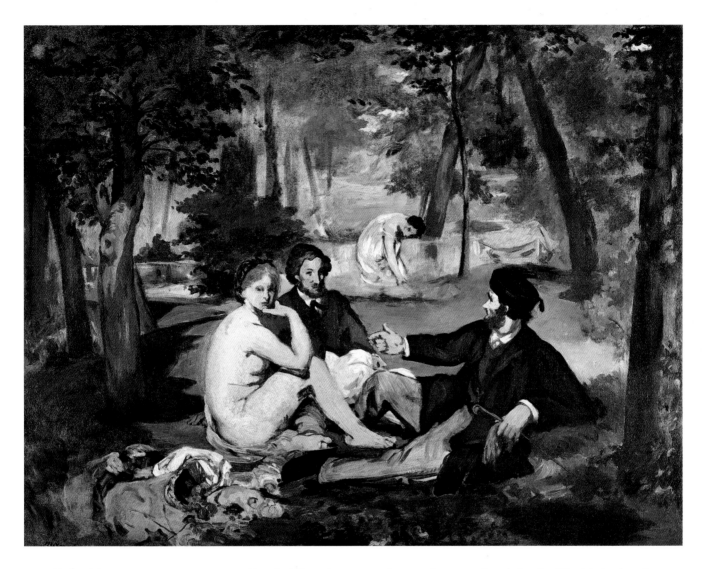

MANET, ÉDOUARD 1832–83
Le Déjeuner sur l'herbe c.1863/7(?)
Oil on canvas, 89.5 x 116.5
Signed, bottom left: 'Manet'

This is a smaller version of the famous
Déjeuner sur l'herbe (Musée d'Orsay, Paris),
which was rejected by the jury of the Paris
Salon in 1863 and exhibited with the title
Le Bain at the Salon des Refusés that year,
causing much controversy.

Manet's friend Antonin Proust recorded
the artist's ambition to rework the theme of
the Titian/Giorgione *Concert champêtre* in
the Louvre in a more luminous, outdoor
ambience; but the final painting was
executed in the studio, apparently based on
studies made on an island in the Seine near
Paris. There are other links with Renaissance
painting; the poses of the principal figures
are based on a group of nymphs and river
gods from an engraving by Marcantonio
Raimondi after Raphael's *Judgment of Paris*.
Manet was also aware of the *fêtes galantes* of

French eighteenth-century painters such as
Antoine Watteau, and of recent popular
romantic prints.

In 1863, the large painting puzzled critics
for several reasons. The juxtaposition of a
naked woman with men in modern dress
was regarded as indecent; the woman's body
was seen as ugly, and the men's clothing,
particularly the smoking-cap of the figure on
the right, led critics to identify them as
students; the handling of the picture did not
give the figures any special status, but treated
them and the background alike, in broad,
vigorous touches of paint. Moreover, it was
unclear what type of subject it was: its very
large dimensions (more than 200 x 250 cm)
led critics to expect a picture with a
significant subject; instead, the viewer was
faced with a risqué scene of modern life,
made all the more provocative by the gaze of
the naked woman, ignoring her companions
and looking directly towards the viewer. In a
sense the work amounted to a parody of
contemporary academic art, treating a scene

from bohemian life with the rhetoric,
and on the scale, of history painting.

The status of the Courtauld version has
been the subject of debate, but X-ray
examination of both canvases has clarified
the issues. The Courtauld picture shows no
significant changes during its execution; the
whole scene was executed very simply and
directly. By contrast, the large version was
considerably altered, having originally
included an open vista with small trees in
its background. It thus seems that the
Courtauld version is a replica, made after the
larger one was completed. The early history
of the painting makes this very plausible,
since its first owner was Manet's friend the
Commandant Lejosne; presumably Lejosne
asked him to make a reduced version of the
subject. The breadth and simplicity of
handling in the Courtauld picture makes it
possible that it was executed a few years after
the large version.   J.H.

Courtauld Collection [P.1932.SC.232]

MANET, ÉDOUARD 1832–83
Banks of the Seine at Argenteuil 1874
Oil on canvas, 62.3 x 103
Signed, bottom left: 'Manet '74'

Banks of the Seine at Argenteuil was painted while Manet was visiting Monet at Argenteuil in the summer of 1874; the models were very probably Monet's wife, Camille, and their seven-year-old son, Jean. Manet had refused to participate in the Impressionists' first group exhibition earlier that year, preferring to continue showing at the Salon, but he was on close personal terms with Monet and gave him much financial help in difficult times.

The picture marks Manet's closest approach to the open-air Impressionism by which the movement is best known, with its broken brushwork and vivid, variegated colour; indeed, it was very probably (in part at least) painted out of doors. But comparison with Monet's *Autumn Effect at Argenteuil* (see p. 85), painted the previous year, reveals important differences. Manet still used clear black paint for certain salient points in the composition – most notably for the ribbons on the back of the woman's hat, and also on the hulls of the boats. Moreover, he did not record the reflections

in the water with any close attention to their actual appearance: the patterns of masts and rigging seen in the water bear little relationship to the forms they reflect, whereas in Monet's paintings, reflections were always closely observed, spreading vertically downwards immediately below the objects reflected. Nor did Manet systematically indicate shadows by the use of colour; we are left with little idea of how the light is falling on the figures.

Strict attention to such notions of naturalism held little value for Manet. Whereas Monet was at this date using the close study of natural effects as the means for rethinking the basic conventions of landscape painting, Manet was primarily concerned with figure subjects, with finding ways of suggesting the unexpected groups that modern people presented in their surroundings. Though the vivid blue of the water in this painting evokes bright summer light, the main focus of the composition is the figures and the boats: the sailing boats in the river, the wash boats along the far bank, and the figures standing inexpressively in front of the view. The factory chimneys seen over the trees echo the lines of the masts and stress the diversity of the scene.

However, in Manet's later work there is

always a tension between the formal organization and pattern of his canvases and their evocation of modernity. Certainly, the broken rhythms and staccato focuses of a picture like the present one can be seen as standing for the nature of experience in the modern world. But, at the same time, the rhythms of the forms – of the masts and boats here, and the play of highlights in the water – can also be read as showing a preoccupation with formal qualities, detached from any representational purpose. It was by focusing on this – on the primacy of the *tache* or patch of colour in Manet's art – that many critics in his lifetime diverted attention from the problematic aspects of his subject matter.

Whereas Monet exhibited many river scenes of similar size, Manet did not show this canvas; as a result of his stay at Argenteuil, he painted two larger, more elaborate scenes of figures by the river which he did submit to the Salon (including *Boating*, Metropolitan Museum of Art, New York). However, he did regard the painting as a fully complete work and sold it to the wealthy collector Ernest May.   J.H.

Private Collection, on extended loan to the Courtauld Gallery

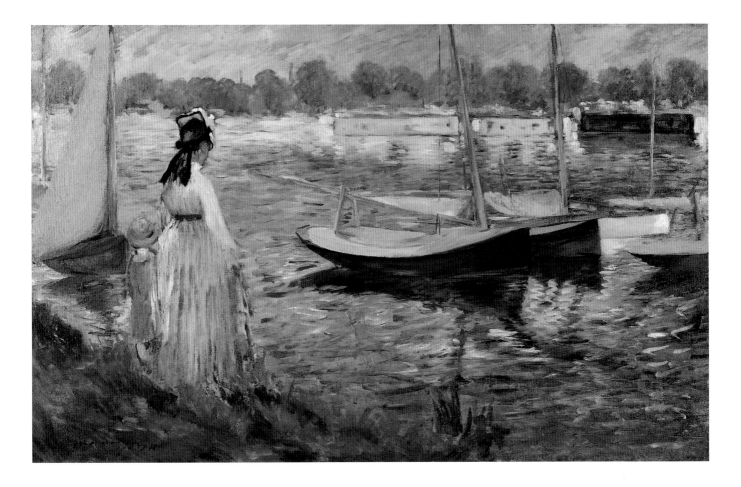

MANET, ÉDOUARD 1832–83
A Bar at the Folies-Bergère 1881–2
Oil on canvas, 96 x 130
Signed on wine-bottle label, bottom left:
'Manet / 1882'

A Bar at the Folies-Bergère was Manet's last major completed painting, exhibited at the Paris Salon in 1882. It shows the interior of one of the most fashionable café-concerts in Paris, but the final painting was executed in Manet's studio, using as a model one of the barmaids who worked at the Folies-Bergère. Georges Jeanniot described Manet at work on the canvas in his studio, with the model posed behind a table laden with bottles and foodstuffs: 'Although he worked from the model, he did not copy nature at all closely; I noted his masterly simplifications. . . . Everything was abbreviated; the tones were made lighter, the colours brighter; the values were more closely related to each other, the tones more contrasting.' Manet insisted that 'conciseness in art was a necessity'.

In the preliminary oil sketch (Private Collection), the barmaid's head is half-turned to the right, with her reflection in the mirror behind the bar in a readily intelligible position, while the reflection of the customer appears near the right-hand edge of the composition, at a lower level. In the final version, the barmaid looks out from the centre of the picture, while her reflection has been displaced much further to the right, and her customer appears in reflection in the extreme top right of the canvas.

In their final form, these reflections cannot be logically understood. The figure of the barmaid is separated much too far from her reflection; in the reflection, the customer is shown close to the barmaid, whereas the viewpoint of the spectator is at some distance from the figure looking out of the picture; and the placing of the bottles in the reflection does not correspond to their position on the bar. X-ray photographs of the painting show that initially its forms were close to those in the sketch, and thus were logically coherent. Substantial changes were made during the execution of the picture, notably the moving of the reflection of the barmaid to the right, and the replacement of the original figure of the customer by the man at the top right. Thus the discrepancies in the final version were introduced deliberately, evolving as Manet worked up the picture. The barmaid becomes the iconic centre of the composition; but a dislocation is created, between her closeness to the man seen in the mirror, and her seeming distance from the viewer.

These distortions of perceived reality would have seemed more unexpected to nineteenth-century viewers than they do today to an eye conditioned by the radical anti-naturalism of much twentieth-century painting. Throughout his career Manet avoided compositions which showed easily legible relationships between figures and presented clear-cut narratives. This can be seen in part as a rejection of the conventions of the fashionable genre painting of the day, but also as an attempt to convey a more vivid sense of actuality, a situation in which relationships between people are rarely clear-cut and unambiguous.

The subject of *A Bar at the Folies-Bergère* enshrined many of the uncertainties of modern urban society. The Folies-Bergère was a popular place of entertainment for fashionable figures in Parisian society and for the *demi-monde*, and prostitutes apparently plied their trade overtly in its foyers and galleries. The status of the barmaids was ambivalent: they were primarily there to serve drinks, but were also potentially available to their clients; thus they might themselves become mere commodities, like the bottles on the bar. Manet's picture seems to evoke this uncertainty.

This feeling is enhanced by the way in which the scene is painted, for the bottles and the fruit bowl on the bar are executed with great richness and finesse, while the figure of the barmaid is more broadly and simply treated. This highlights the barmaid's merchandise, the primary reason for her presence behind the bar, and thus brings out the ambivalence of her own status in the transactions she enacts.

Twentieth-century writing about Manet has until recently tended to favour formalist explanations of the structure of Manet's paintings, arguing that he was primarily concerned with aesthetic questions about form and colour. However, as originally displayed at the Paris Salon, these works presented a systematic challenge to the prevailing conventions of representation and the coherence of the world which such conventions created; Manet's art challenged social as well as artistic values.   J.H.

Courtauld Collection [P.1934.SC.234]

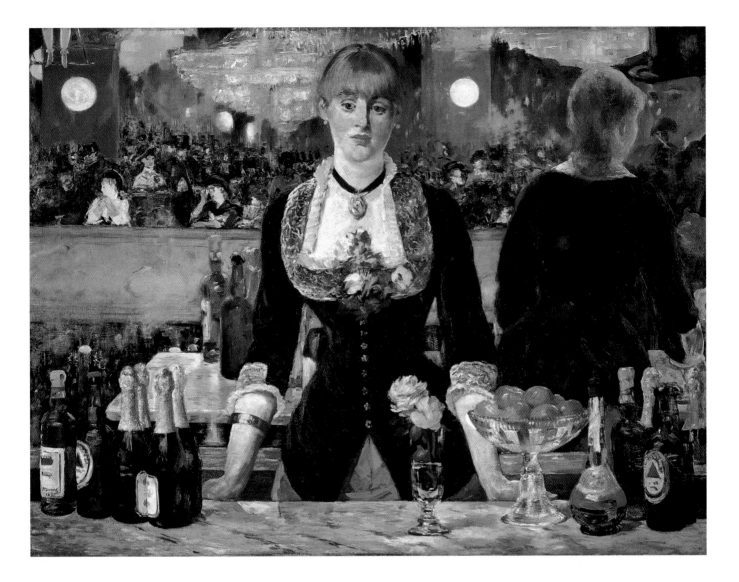

DEGAS, EDGAR 1834–1917
Two Dancers on the Stage 1874
Oil on canvas, 61.5 x 46
Signed, bottom left: 'Degas'

This composition is closely related to a group of three pictures that show dancers rehearsing on a clearly defined stage, with other waiting dancers and a ballet master. Here, though, Degas concentrated on the two figures, without indicating whether we are watching a performance or a rehearsal. Our attention is focused on their poses, as seen from the unexpected angle of a box virtually above the edge of the stage.

Although the figures are shown in standard ballet positions and their gestures suggest some sort of interchange, the viewer is given no clue as to the narrative being enacted. Any attempt to see this as a coherent, framed grouping is also undermined by the appearance, at the far left, of a third dancer, her figure cut by the frame; her presence challenges any attempt to understand the gestures of the other two.

There is a paradoxical relationship between the elegance of the dancers' poses and their snub-nosed facial features. Contemporary notions of physiognomy, in which Degas was much interested, saw a correlation between facial appearance and personality; physiognomies such as these were associated with a lower order of human development, and with the lower classes. Degas regularly gave such features to the dancers in his paintings, as if to emphasize the contrast between the humble working-class girls who made up the *corps de ballet*, and the finesse that the discipline of classical ballet imposed on them.

Degas always presented the ballet in ways which revealed its artificiality, by including other elements – figures who do not watch the dancers, or dancers who play no part in the main action, like the figure on the left here. His interest in this theme was part of his attempt in the 1870s to study the visible world from many angles which had not been sanctioned in previous art, but which seemed to him characteristic of the ways in which everyday life appeared in the modern city.

Degas exhibited a similarly treated composition in which this pairing of figures appears (now Musée d'Orsay, Paris) at the first Impressionist group exhibition in 1874, and that painting, together with the present canvas, makes an interesting contrast to the bold colour and brushwork with which the Impressionist group is usually associated. The stage-flats in *Two Dancers on the Stage* are treated in free dabs of colour, but the figures are modelled with comparative delicacy. The overall colour scheme is quite subdued, with vivid points of pink, yellow and green on the figures' shoes, flowers, bodices and head-dresses.   J.H.

Courtauld Collection [P.1934.SC.89]

76

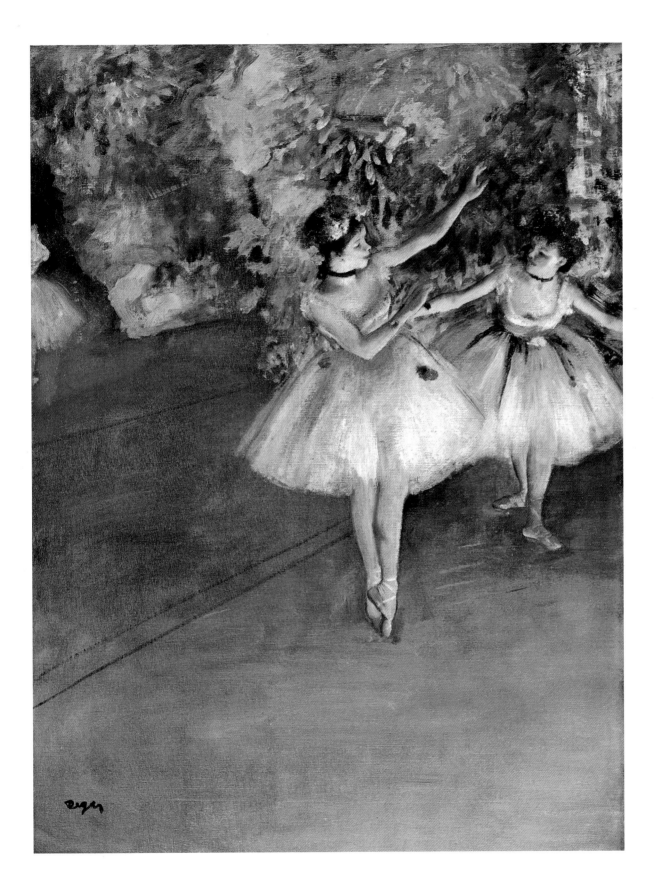

DEGAS, EDGAR 1834–1917
After the Bath, Woman Drying Herself
c.1895(?)
Bound pastel on paper, 67.7 x 57.8
Stamped bottom left with mark of Degas's studio sale

The subject of women bathing in tubs or drying themselves first appeared in Degas's monotypes c.1880, and became one of the artist's recurring themes in his late work.

At the eighth Impressionist group exhibition in 1886, Degas showed a set of pastels under the collective title *Sequence of Nudes of Women Bathing, Washing, Drying, Wiping Themselves, Combing their Hair or Having it Combed*. The present work, *After the Bath, Woman Drying Herself*, was probably executed some years later than this series. A number of other drawings are closely related to the Courtauld pastel, but its place in this complex sequence of evolving images is as yet unclear. The series, however, vividly illustrates Degas's dictum : 'Make a drawing, begin it again, trace it; begin it again and trace again.'

Degas began to draw *After the Bath, Woman Drying Herself* on the upper of the two sheets of thin, smooth, machine-made paper which make up the composition's support. After a bold initial drawing in black chalk, Degas blocked in substantial areas of the sheet with broad, open strokes of pink-red pastel. At an early stage in the drawing campaign, the composition was extended at the bottom by adding a second strip of paper. At this point, too, all the edges of the composition were trimmed, and the sheets were laid down on thin card. Sometime after completion, the drawing and card support were mounted on stout millboard.

The texture of the pastel in virtually all areas of this drawing indicates that it has been bound. The pale-yellow towel on the chair has a dense, paste-like surface, suggesting that the pastel may in part have been applied with the brush. Its surface is furrowed by zigzag striations associated with strokes of yellow: it is possible that these were drawn with a stick of bound pastel which had become dried and hardened. A similarly hardened black pastel or crayon seems to have been used for lines defining the model's spine and ribcage, which equally have been incised into the sheet. In other areas, pastel or chalk has been applied either moist, or in a liquid state. The spattered appearance of the black shadow on the chair to the right of the towel indicates that it has been brushed or wiped on, while the blacks, yellows and touches of red in the hair have been dabbed in with a rag, or perhaps, for the smaller touches, with the finger tips. Stippling in the bather's wrist and raised left hand, and on the rim of the bath at the right, is applied with the moist point of the pastel, as are the delicately stroked diagonals which model the interior of the tub. In other parts of the composition, such as the edges of the towel with which the bather dries herself, her neck, raised arm and back, the pastel is heavily impacted – indeed, almost encrusted – on the paper's surface in dense hatchings, or in screens of vigorous zigzags.

The figure is modelled by meshed veils of V-shaped hatching in blacks, white, Indian red, and a tender pink contrasted with pale olive. For the most part, the hatching follows the planes of the torso: however, in the right shoulder – an area Degas extensively revised – sharp raking lines affirming the new form also cut across it,

denying its three-dimensionality. The cool, nuanced tones of flesh, bath and towels are surrounded by the intense, hot colours of wall, carpets and chair.

Despite the informality of the model's pose, the composition is carefully organized both spatially and as a linear framework. The bather's left upper arm and thighs are aligned with the diagonals of the bathtub, skirting board and carpet, while the left forearm, linked with the top left of the sheet, is echoed at the upper right by the form of the curtain: the curves of the bath towel, chairback and tub resonate with the rounded form of the woman's back. Throughout the composition, too, Degas modified the forms as the work progressed, and at certain points, for instance the right knee, the forms remain unresolved. As with nearly all of Degas's later drawings, this work was abandoned in a provisional state.

In the mid-1880s Degas told George Moore that his aims in his pictures of bathing women were to show

a human creature preoccupied with herself – a cat who licks herself: hitherto, the nude has always been represented in poses which presuppose an audience, but these women of mine are honest and simple folk, unconcerned by any other interests than those involved in their physical condition. It is as if you looked through a key-hole.

Images such as these have at times been seen as misogynist, by critics from J.K. Huysmans onwards, but they show the same studied detachment of viewpoint as his treatment of many other themes. There is no hint of savagery in the way that his models are presented.   W.B.

Courtauld Collection [P.1932.SC.27]

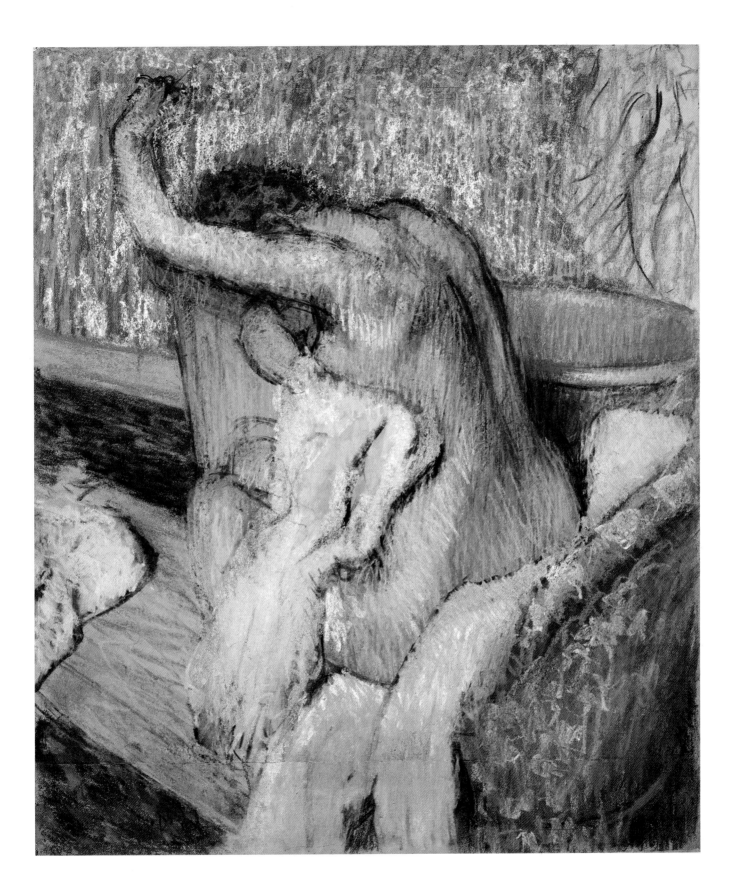

MORISOT, BERTHE 1841–95
Portrait of a Woman c.1872
Oil on canvas, 56 x 46.1
Signed, top left: 'B. Morisot'

For some years this painting was thought to be a portrait of the artist's sister, Edma, who was certainly Morisot's favourite model during the 1860s and 1870s. The two sisters were particularly close, partly because both had defied conventional expectations of women of their social class, having taken their practice of painting beyond that of a polite, drawing-room accomplishment. However, their activities were still constrained by social propriety: it was thought unseemly for an unmarried woman to paint a portrait of a man to whom she was not related, hence Morisot repeatedly painted women, children and members of her family. Morisot's continued doubts about her own abilities also made her disinclined to paint people other than members of her family; she wrote in a letter, 'Decidedly I am too nervous to make anyone sit for me.'

However, in spite of these factors which suggest that this may be a portrait of Edma Morisot (Madame Pontillon after she married in 1869), it remains true that there is no evidence to confirm the sitter's identity. Count Seilern, who acquired the painting for his own collection, identified the sitter as Edma by comparing the features seen here with those in other works by Morisot which are known to show her sister, including a striking pastel portrait (now in the Louvre) of Edma drawn only a few weeks before she gave birth to her first child. This is, nevertheless, a notoriously unreliable way of identifying sitters, since it involves personal opinions which are difficult or impossible to corroborate. There are aspects of this woman's face – her cleft chin, large eyes and lack of high cheekbones – which differ markedly from other portraits of Edma, so it may be that the identification of the sitter proposed by the authors of the catalogue raisonné of Morisot's work, published in 1961, is correct. They called her 'Madame Heudé', but, since nothing so far has been discovered about this woman, their identification also remains provisional.

The formality of the sitter's pose would be appropriate for someone outside Morisot's immediate family, although the application of paint, which ranges from broad sweeps of the brush to delicately but still freely applied strokes describing the frills and lace of the woman's clothes, shows the interests that Morisot shared with the painters she was to exhibit alongside in the first Impressionist exhibition in Paris in 1874.   S.H.

Princes Gate Collection [P.1978.PG.279]

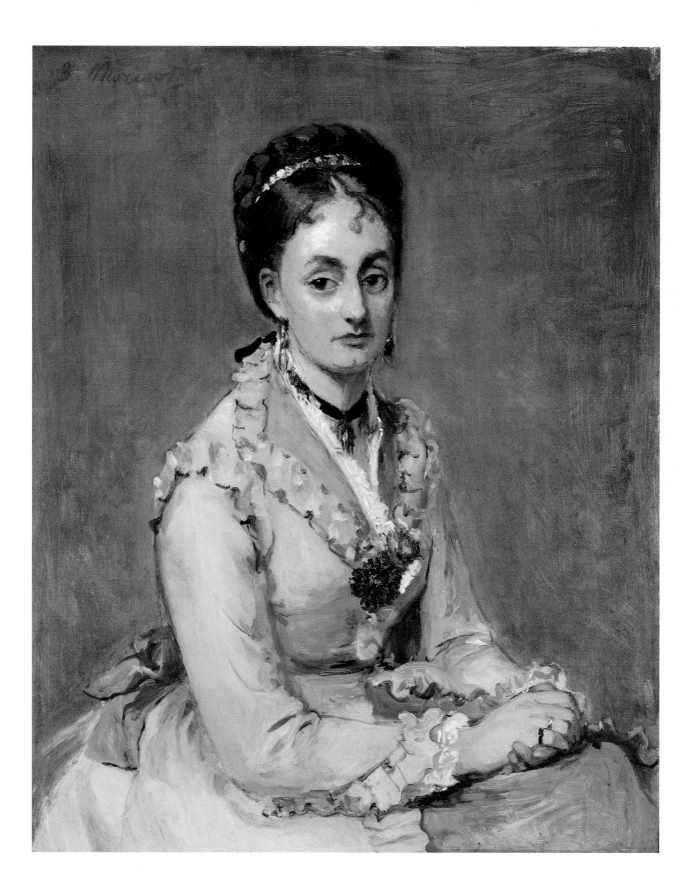

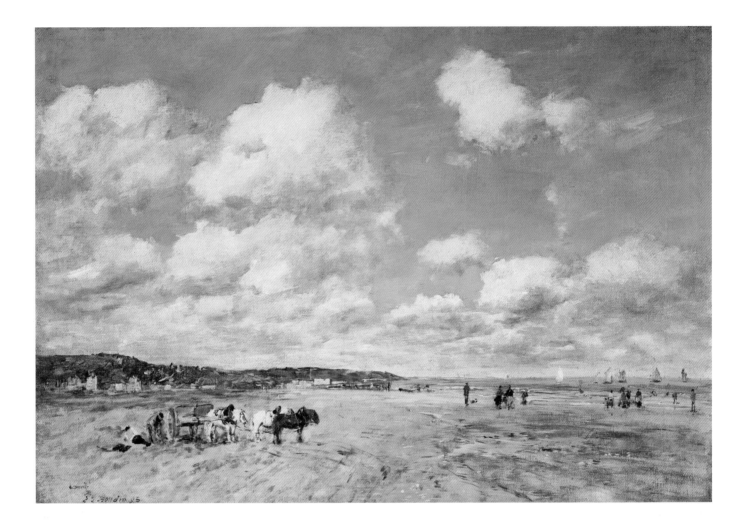

BOUDIN, EUGÈNE 1824–98
Deauville 1893
Oil on canvas, 50.8 x 74.2
Signed, bottom left: 'Deauville / E. Boudin 93'

In his later work, Boudin concentrated more on the open panoramas of the Normandy beaches than on the local holidaymakers. The figures here are rapidly indicated, with holidaymakers, it seems, over by the water, and a group of working men with their cart and horses on the left, so that we have a sense of the varied uses of the beach. But light and atmosphere form the principal subject of the painting.

Boudin had worked closely with Monet and had exhibited in the first Impressionist group exhibition in 1874, but he never fully adopted the broken touch and lavish atmospheric colour of the Impressionists. His brushwork was tighter and more graphic, delicately suggesting forms and textures; and his colour remained more restrained, though nuances of blue and green here suggest the forms in the distance, and a sequence of tiny red touches adds extra animation to the background.

By this refined touch and colour, Boudin evoked the vast scale of the beach and sky, revealing the skills which led Corot to name him the 'king of skies'. However, the execution of the canvas was evidently more complex than appears at first sight; the original painting of the sky was largely removed before Boudin completed the work in its present form.   J.H.

Courtauld Collection [P.1948.SC.44]

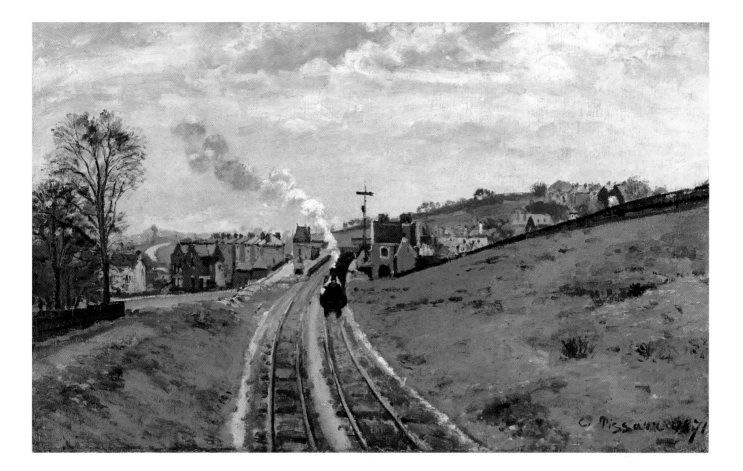

PISSARRO, CAMILLE 1830–1903
Lordship Lane Station, Dulwich 1871
Oil on canvas, 44.5 x 72.5
Signed, bottom right: 'C. Pissarro 1871'

Pissarro painted this picture while living in London, a refugee from the Franco-Prussian War of 1870–1. It represents Lordship Lane Station (now demolished) on the old Crystal Palace (High Level) Railway, seen from the footbridge across the cutting to the south of the station. The line was opened in 1865 to cater for visitors to the Crystal Palace, very popular as a recreation and exhibition centre since its reconstruction in Sydenham in 1852–4. The scene shows a modern landscape in the making, with new houses punctuating still-undeveloped open land.

The chosen subject is deliberately anti-picturesque, with rough slopes and drab fences framing the central motif of tracks and train; the scrubby terrain on the right takes up almost a quarter of the picture. X-ray photographs show that there was originally a figure, perhaps holding a scythe, on the bank to the right; by erasing it, Pissarro removed the only feature of any obvious pictorial interest in this area.

This canvas seems to be the first occasion on which an artist from the Impressionist group adopted a train as his central motif. It may echo Turner's famous *Rain, Steam and Speed*, which Pissarro saw in the National Gallery in London, but, in place of Turner's lavish atmospherics, Pissarro adopted a far more detached view, closer in its treatment to topographical prints of the new railway landscape. The signal, silhouetted in the centre, can be seen as a secularized equivalent of a crucifix – a rejection of traditional elevated subject matter in the search for the truly contemporary.

The picture is quite subdued in colour; the effect of an overcast day is evoked by varied greens and soft red-browns, with the white of the smoke and the clear black of the locomotive as a central focus. This comparatively tonal treatment, with nuances of a restricted range of colours, is in marked contrast to the lavish colour which, soon afterwards, Monet and Pissarro began to adopt in sunlit scenes. The brushwork is softly variegated to suggest the different textures, stressing the diversity of the elements that make up this characteristically modern landscape. By contrast, twelve years later at Rouen, Pissarro subordinated the elements in an industrial scene (see p. 84) to an overall play of coloured touches. This change, from a concentration on the distinctive elements in a subject to a preoccupation with overall unifying effects of light, is fundamental to the development of Impressionism in these years.   J.H.

Courtauld Collection [P.1948.SC.317]

83

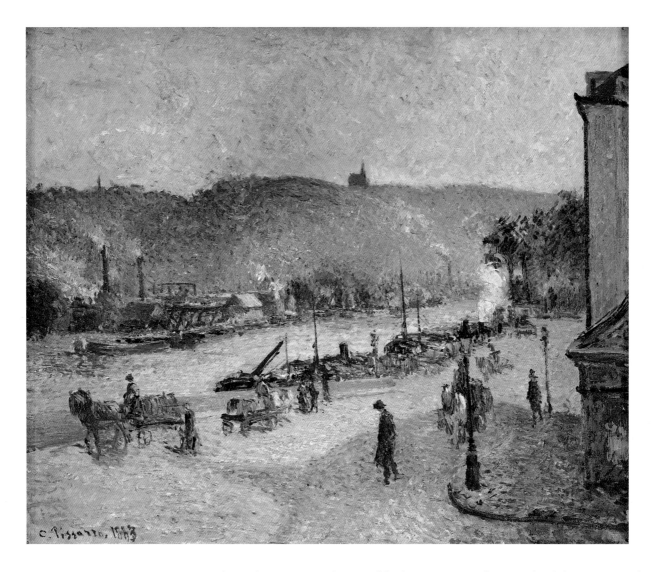

PISSARRO, CAMILLE 1830–1903
The Quays at Rouen 1883
Oil on canvas, 46.3 x 55.7
Signed, bottom left: 'C. Pissarro, 1883'

Pissarro spent three months at Rouen in autumn 1883, concentrating on industrial and commercial scenes along the banks of the Seine. Here, the view is to the east from the Ile Lacroix, with factories at the base of the Côte Sainte-Catherine across the river, and, silhouetted against the sky, the church of Notre-Dame de Bonsecours, a Neo-Gothic structure of 1840–2, celebrated as a pilgrimage centre.

The raised viewpoint, above and somewhat distanced from the scene, is characteristic of Pissarro's treatment of urban subjects. By contrast, in his contemporary scenes of peasants in the countryside, he adopted a closer viewpoint, integrating the figures more fully with their surroundings. His very different treatment of these two themes perhaps expresses the contrasts that

he saw between city and country life: the countryside is shown as the repository of a harmonious way of life, while the activities of the city are more distanced from each other – life is detached from labour. However, there is nothing in this painting, either in the subject or in the way it is treated, which makes any overt social criticism or judgment; all the elements in the subject are integrated into an overall harmony; church and factories, boats, carts and figures are all given equal significance in the ensemble.

The handling of the picture is particularly unified, with virtually every area built up from successions of small dabs and dashes of colour which give the work a constantly mobile surface; this allows Pissarro to introduce variations of colour throughout, so as to evoke the play of coloured light and atmosphere. Though each area has a dominant colour, small touches of other colours recur, and these relate to other areas of the picture, linking lit and shadowed

areas, foreground and distance; across the whole, too, small very light-toned accents create flecks of light which enliven the entire picture. With these calculated devices, Pissarro suggested the effect of the unifying hazy sunlight.

Pissarro began with a simpler, flatter lay-in before elaborating the surface. The final touches refine the effect and give the surface a distinctive rhythm, which is comparable to, though less rigid than, the parallel strokes which Cézanne applied to his more highly finished paintings at this date. In Pissarro's Rouen paintings, this refinement of the surface took place, in part at least, in his studio; following his return from Rouen, he wrote: 'Result of my trip: I return with pleasure to my studio, and look over my studies with greater indulgence, with a better idea of what needs to be done to them.' J.H.

Courtauld Collection [P.1932.SC.319]

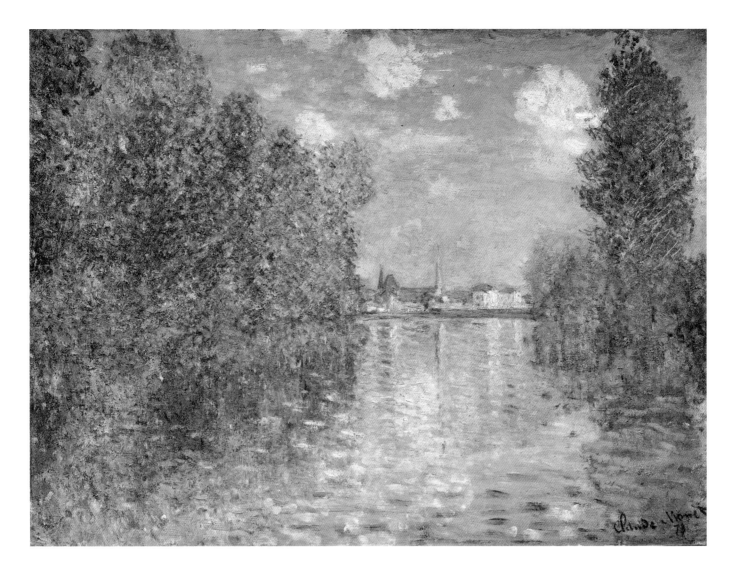

MONET, CLAUDE 1840–1926
Autumn Effect at Argenteuil 1873
Oil on canvas, 55 x 74.5
Signed, bottom right: 'Claude Monet / 73'

The town of Argenteuil, in the background, is seen from a side branch of the river Seine; the bold blue stripe running across the centre of the canvas represents the main channel of the river. At this period Argenteuil was expanding, both as an industrial town and as a centre for recreational sailing. Often Monet would present contemporary facets of the place; in some views from the same branch of the river modern houses are shown on the bank to the right. Here, however, the scene has a timeless quality, with a few houses presided over by a church spire, framed by the splendour of the sunlit trees.

The picture corresponds closely to Frederick Wedmore's description of a canvas shown in the first major Impressionist exhibition held in London, at Dowdeswell's

Gallery in 1883: '. . . palpitating light and golden hue. The whole one side of the canvas is filled with flame-coloured autumn trees which throw their bright reflection of a rosier flame-colour upon a broad river-water otherwise turquoise and coral.'

Of all Monet's paintings of the period, this one most completely abandons traditional methods of chiaroscuro modelling, by gradations from dark to light tones, in favour of a composition based on clear colours, which model form and evoke space. The picture is dominated by the bold contrast between orange and blue, but the glowing bank of trees is built up from constantly varied warm hues; on the right, soft clear blues indicate the shadows in the trees. As often in his landscapes, Monet avoided a direct perspectival lead into the pictorial space, in favour of an open-fronted view across water; recession into space is suggested by the blues on the far buildings, together with the diminishing scale of the brush-strokes in the water.

The brushwork is very varied, ranging from the use of broad, firm strokes in the foreground reflections, which anchor the whole composition, to the little dabs and hooks of colour in the shaded side of the tree on the right. The treatment of the scattered clouds is particularly freely improvised. In the trees, the paint surface seems almost encrusted. At a late stage in the execution of the picture, Monet scraped away some of this paint in long crisp strokes, probably made with the handle of a brush; these are most clearly visible on the right-hand tree, where the strokes removed the whole depth of the paint layer, so revealing the very light-grey priming; however, they also appear throughout the foliage of the trees on the left. Presumably Monet was dissatisfied with the density of the paint layers, but such scraping is an extremely unusual feature in his work.   J.H.

Courtauld Collection [P.1932.SC.274]

85

MONET, CLAUDE 1840–1926
Vase of Flowers c.1881–2
Oil on canvas, 100.4 x 81.8
Signed, bottom right: 'Claude Monet'

Between 1878 and 1882, for the only time in his career, Monet concentrated on still lifes, alongside his painting of landscapes. In these years he was beginning to find a more regular market for his paintings, and he was able to sell still lifes more readily and for higher prices than landscapes; when the dealer Durand-Ruel began to buy his landscapes regularly from 1881 onwards, he soon virtually gave up still-life painting. *Vase of Flowers*, a picture of a lavish display of Wild Mallow, very probably belongs to the last still lifes that he undertook in this phase, a group of particularly large flower paintings, which, as his letters show, caused him great trouble.

The final state of *Vase of Flowers* reveals his difficulties. Although it is densely and elaborately worked, Monet did not complete it for sale at the time of its execution. It was one of many paintings from earlier years which he signed and sold in the last years of his life.

In contrast to the paintings which Monet completed for sale in the 1880s (such as *Chrysanthemums*, in the Metropolitan Museum of Art, New York, another of the same group of still lifes), the forms of the leaves and flowers in his *Vase of Flowers* are less crisply handled, treated in rapid dabs and dashes of colour which, though complex, do not always define the forms clearly. In his still lifes of these years Monet was presenting lavish displays of flowers and fruit in ways which avoided the more rigid, structured conventions of still-life painting in the tradition of the eighteenth-century French painter Chardin; but on this occasion he did not succeed in finding a fully resolved pictorial form for this mass of blooms and greenery. The vigorous, but slightly crude and even disorderly touch which features in this work is more akin to twentieth-century tastes than it would have been to those of the buyers of Monet's paintings in the 1880s. J.H.

Courtauld Collection [P.1932.SC.275]

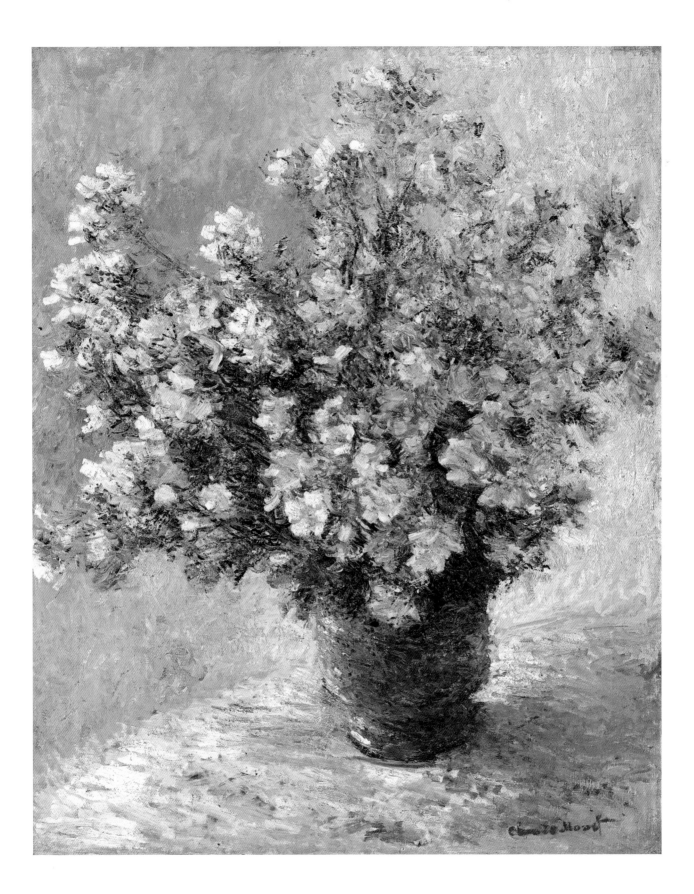

MONET, CLAUDE 1840–1926
Antibes 1888
Oil on canvas, 65.5 x 92.4
Signed, bottom left: 'Claude Monet 88'

Monet worked at Antibes in early 1888, and on his return to Paris exhibited ten paintings of the area at the gallery of the dealers Boussod & Valadon, run by Theo van Gogh, brother of the painter. *Antibes* was probably one of these.

When painting the Mediterranean coast, Monet was faced with the problem of capturing the intensity of southern light and colour. He wrote to Berthe Morisot from Antibes: 'It's so difficult, so tender and so delicate, while I am so inclined to brutality.' In a letter to his partner Alice Hoschedé, he commented: 'What I bring back from here will be sweetness itself, white, pink and blue, all enveloped in this magical air.' Monet evoked the effect of the southern light by heightening his colours and by co-ordinating the colour relationships throughout the picture, into clear sequences of contrasts. Here, greens and blues are set against sharp accents of pink, red and orange, with related colours recurring all over the canvas. Late

in the execution of the painting, he stressed the warm end of its colour range, by adding little touches of red and orange across the distant mountains and on the foliage of the tree, and by adding his signature in a bold red-orange shade.

Although it suggests a passing effect of outdoor light, the painting is elaborately executed and was much reworked. X-ray examination shows that the sea was originally executed far more boldly, perhaps showing an effect of strong wind, whereas the delicate final strokes applied on the water surface suggest calmer conditions. Monet also moved the position of the tree-trunk a little to the left, and many of the crisp touches on the edges of the foliage were added at a late stage, after the initial painting of the sky had had time to dry. Some of these adjustments may have been made at Antibes, but by this date Monet felt that the finishing touches on a painting, added to give the picture an overall coherence, needed to be made in the studio.

The composition of *Antibes*, with its silhouetted tree and open sides, reflects Monet's interest in Japanese woodblock prints, of which he was an avid collector.

In the 1880s he travelled widely, exploring subjects which showed the most extreme natural effects, and his knowledge of Japanese art helped him to find ways of formulating these scenes in pictorial terms.

Vincent van Gogh was not in Paris when his brother exhibited Monet's Antibes paintings, but the Australian painter J.P. Russell wrote to him about the exhibition. Vincent relayed Russell's reactions back to his brother, mentioning a painting that is probably the present canvas:

[Russell] criticizes the Monets very ably, begins by liking them very much, the attack on the problem, the enfolding tinted air, the colour. After that he shows what there is to find fault with – the total lack of construction, for instance one of his trees will have far too much foliage for the thickness of the trunk, and so always and everywhere from the standpoint of the reality of things, from the standpoint of natural *laws*, he is exasperating enough. He ends by saying that this quality of attacking the difficulties is what everyone ought to have.

J.H.

Courtauld Collection [P.1948.SC.276]

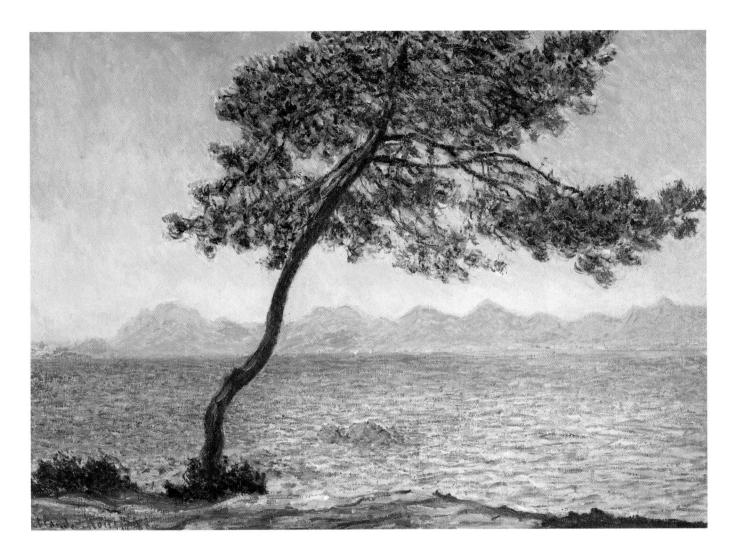

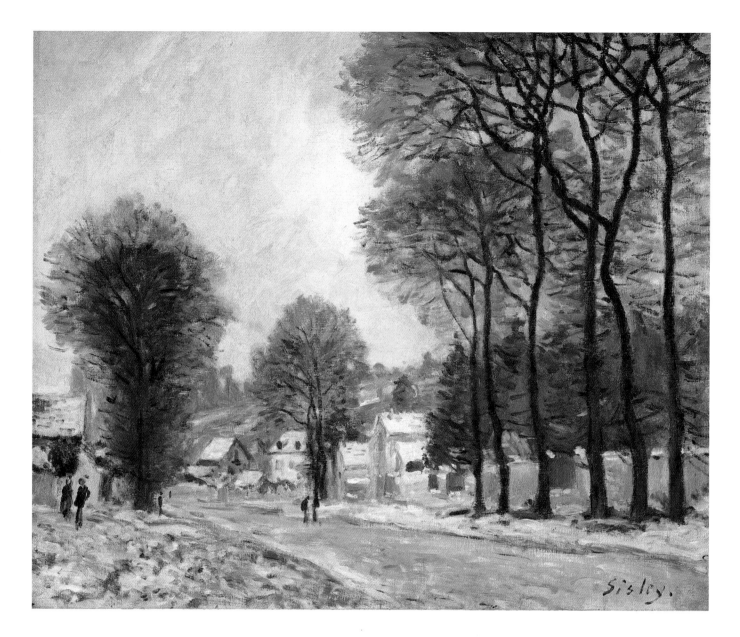

SISLEY, ALFRED 1839–99
Snow at Louveciennes 1874
Oil on canvas, 46.3 x 55.8
Signed, bottom right: 'Sisley.'

The village of Louveciennes lies near the river Seine, about 10 miles (16 km) west of Paris; Sisley painted many views of this area in the 1870s, and both Monet and Pissarro also worked there. Here, the subject is a simple, everyday scene, of no obvious picturesque potential: humble houses set along a road, with an uninviting foreground – a rough verge, an open road, tree-trunks and a stretch of wall. The figures provide a sense of scale, but, because they are treated very summarily and placed in the middle distance, do little to characterize the scene. It is by the delicacy of the atmospheric effects – by the nuances of colour and touch – that Sisley gave this outwardly unprepossessing scene its pictorial interest.

Although the tonality of the painting is comparatively subdued, and the trees to the right and left give it a dark-toned frame, the effect of an overcast winter day is evoked by soft variations of colour; the blues across the distant hills and houses are set against the soft creams and beiges of the road and nearer buildings. The paint is quite thin throughout the picture; more broadly painted areas alternate with zones built up from successions of varied smaller touches, like the broken accents across the verge at the bottom left. Though the brushwork has no dominant rhythm, the soft variegations of touch and colour give the whole painting a freshness and mobility. The light-toned priming of the canvas shows through the paint at many points and heightens the effect of luminosity.

In 1875 Sisley painted a second picture of precisely the same subject, this time in summer, but there is no evidence to show that he intended the two works to be seen as a pair.   J.H.

Courtauld Collection [P.1932.SC.409]

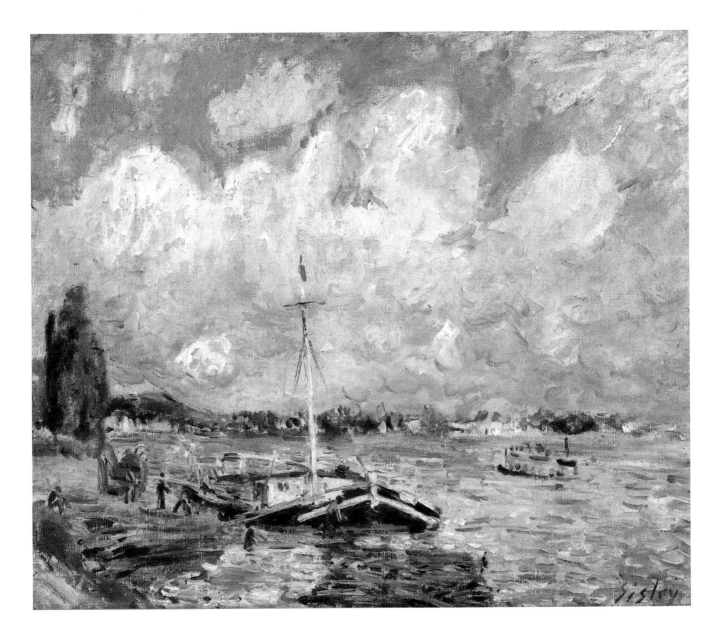

SISLEY, ALFRED 1839–99
Boats on the Seine c.1877
Oil on canvas, laid down on plywood,
37.2 x 44.3
Signed, bottom right: 'Sisley'

This canvas is smaller and more sketchily
treated than most Impressionist paintings of
the 1870s, but the fact that it is signed shows
that Sisley regarded it as a complete work in
its own right. Throughout the decade, the
landscapists of the group painted rapid
sketches such as this alongside more
elaborated canvases; the sketches were
particularly appreciated by fellow artists
and the most 'artistic' of collectors, whereas
their more highly worked pictures were
more likely to find ready buyers through the
dealer market.

By 1877, Sisley's brushwork had become
more broken and energetic (cf. *Snow at
Louveciennes*, opposite); the whole scene
is animated by hooks, dashes and streaks of
colour which capture with great vigour the
effect of a sunny, breezy day. Little figures
can be distinguished on the near bank, but
they are not differentiated from the other
elements around them. However, for all the
picture's apparent speed of execution, the
light and weather on a day such as this must
have changed far too quickly for Sisley to
capture the effect immediately; completing
the picture must have involved a complex
act of memory and synthesis, in order to
evoke so fresh an effect.

The light-toned canvas priming, visible in
many places, enhances the work's luminosity,
but the true highlights of the picture are the

vigorous white accents in the clouds and on
the barges and the far houses. Even the
darkest tones in the scene – on the barge and
the river bank – are coloured, in deep blues
and reds, and distance is suggested by blues
set against the green foliage and the sharp
red accents of the roofs. These warm accents,
picked up elsewhere, act as an important
contrast to the dominant blues and greens,
and sharpen the overall colour effect.

The subject, the unloading of wood from
a river barge, with a passing passenger-ferry
on the river, is explicitly contemporary,
presenting the Seine at Billancourt (on the
south-western outskirts of Paris) not as a
rural retreat but as a commercial and
recreational waterway.   J.H.

Courtauld Collection [P.1948.SC.410]

91

RENOIR, PIERRE-AUGUSTE
1841–1919
The Theatre Box (La Loge) 1874
Oil on canvas, 80 x 63.5
Signed, bottom left: 'A. Renoir 74'

The artist's brother Edmond and Nini, a model from Montmartre, posed for this painting, which was one of Renoir's prime exhibits at the first group exhibition of the Impressionists in Paris in 1874. It was at this exhibition that the comments of critics about Monet's *Impression, Sunrise* (Musée Marmottan, Paris) led to the group being named 'Impressionists'. However, *The Theatre Box* is very different from Monet's rapid sketch, and far more elaborated than some of Renoir's other exhibits at this show; he continued throughout his career to paint elaborate, highly finished canvases like this one, alongside less formal works.

Yet the technique of *The Theatre Box* is very varied and fluent; forms are delicately and softly brushed without crisp contours, and the execution of the model's bodice and the flowers on it is a particularly virtuoso display. Her face, though, is executed more minutely, its modelling more fully suggested by soft and varied colour; the viewer's eye moves from bodice to face in search of the principal focus of the composition. The model's gown, with its bold stripes, gives the composition a strong black and white structure; actual black paint is used here, though often mixed with blue to suggest the play of light and shade across it. Around its bold pattern, varied nuances of blue, green and yellow are set against the warm hues of her flesh and the pinks and reds in the flowers on her bodice and hair.

The subject of the theatre box was a favoured one among painters of modern Parisian life during the 1870s. Here, Renoir plays on the contrast between the poses of the two figures: the woman looks out with her opera glasses beside her in her hand, as if to receive the gaze of other members of the audience, while her male companion looks through his opera glasses out from the box and upwards, and thus implicitly at the occupant of another box, not down at the stage. The implied position of the viewer within the theatre is uncertain; the figures seem to be quite close, yet we are clearly outside the front edge of the box.

In his treatment of his model, Renoir left her exact social and sexual status ambiguous; one of the reviewers of the first group exhibition (where the canvas was well received) described her as a typical *cocotte* (a kept woman), and humorously used her as a warning to young girls of their fate if they were waylaid by fashion and vanity, while another saw her as 'a figure from the world of elegance'. In his paintings Renoir generally eschewed clear signs of social and moral difference; unlike Manet in *A Bar at the Folies-Bergère* (see p. 75), he never painted images that might appear to suggest any social uncertainty or division, but presented all aspects of modern Parisian life in the 1870s as if they were equally harmonious and untroubled.   J.H.

Courtauld Collection [P.1948.SC.338]

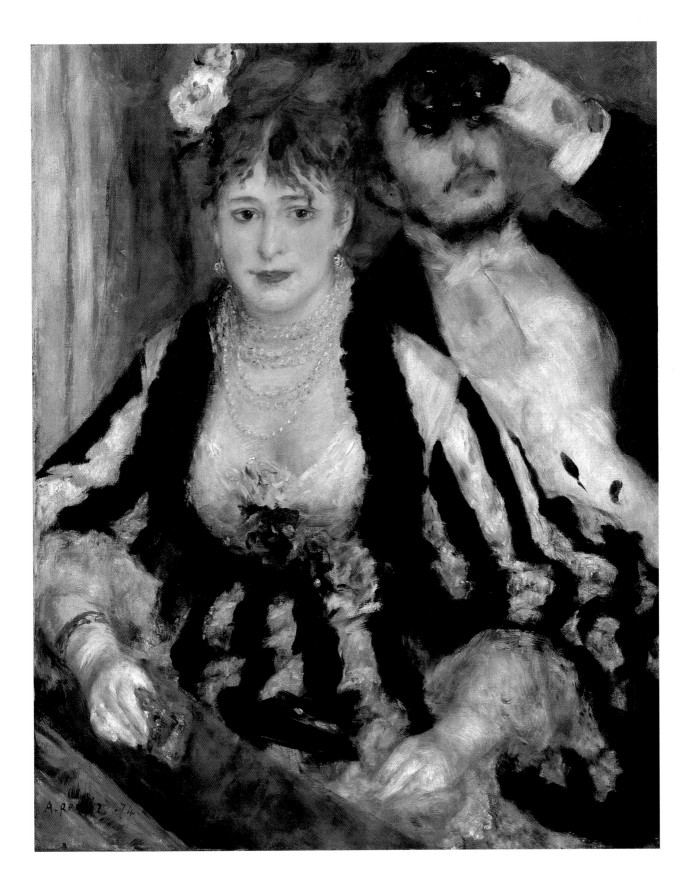

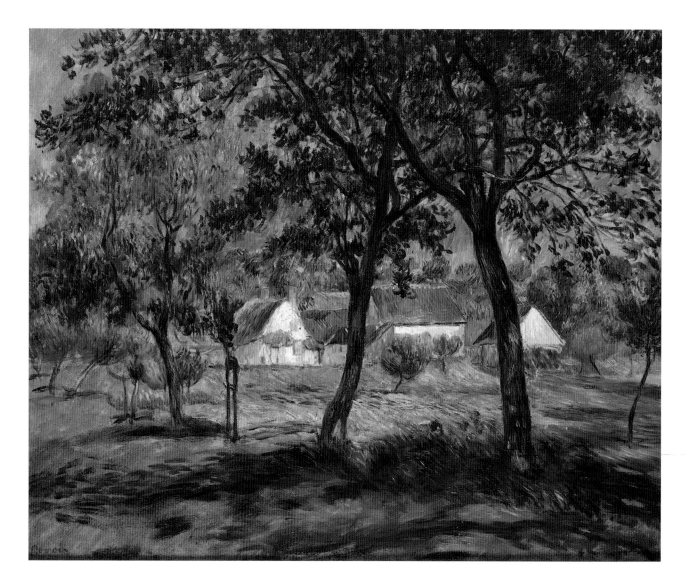

RENOIR, PIERRE-AUGUSTE
1841–1919
The Outskirts of Pont-Aven c.1892
Oil on canvas, 54.5 x 65
Signed, bottom left: 'Renoir'

Renoir's only documented visits to Pont-Aven in Brittany were in 1892 and 1893, though he had also travelled to Brittany in 1891. The back of the stretcher of *The Outskirts of Pont-Aven* bears a note 'Pont.Aven 1887', but the treatment of the subject makes it much more likely that the painting belongs to the early 1890s. Although Renoir's visits to Pont-Aven did not coincide with Gauguin's time there (see *The Haystacks*, p. 105), in 1892 he did meet some of Gauguin's former associates, such as Emile Bernard and Armand Séguin.

The treatment of the scene reflects the period of technical experimentation that Renoir went through in the years from around 1881 into the early 1890s. Much of the foreground is loosely brushed in with fluid paint, in a manner similar to his landscapes of around 1880. But the tree-trunks are far more crisply defined, and the foliage is treated in small emphatic strokes of colour. This concern with the definition of forms is an indication of Renoir's feelings of dissatisfaction, during the 1880s, with the sketch-like quality and formlessness of Impressionist technique. The small tight brush-strokes on the foliage probably reflect the example of Cézanne, with whom Renoir worked on several occasions during the 1880s (see *The Montagne Sainte Victoire*, p. 111).

In *The Outskirts of Pont-Aven*, Renoir also introduced a wide range of vivid atmospheric colour. The background is dominated by intense contrasts of green and red-orange, and forms a luminous backdrop to the crisp silhouettes of the trees in the foreground, but even these are full of colour, suggesting the play of sun through the foliage and on to the tree-trunks and branches.

The forms of the houses seen in the background are characteristic of Brittany, but, beyond this, Renoir did little here to evoke the habitual visual associations – the distinctive regional dress and local customs that were the focus of so many paintings of Brittany in the later nineteenth century (cf. Gauguin, *The Haystacks*). J.H.

Princes Gate Collection [P.1978.PG.339]

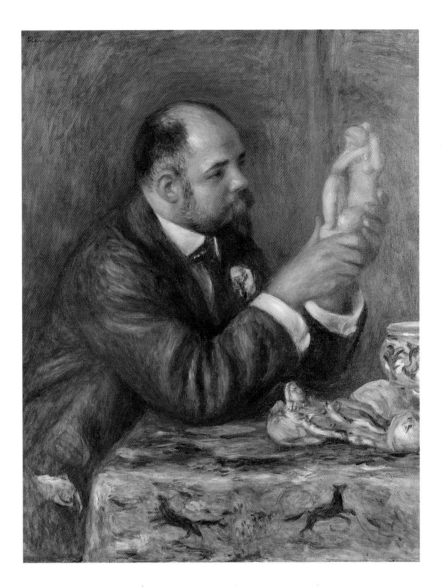

RENOIR, PIERRE-AUGUSTE
1841–1919
Portrait of Ambroise Vollard 1908
Oil on canvas, 81.6 x 65.2
Signed, top left: 'Renoir. 08'

Renoir first met Vollard around 1895. Born on the island of Réunion in 1868, Vollard became as a dealer in Paris and began to buy from Renoir. After 1900 he became one of the principal dealers in Renoir's paintings, though, in retrospect, his main claim to fame is as the organizer, from 1895, of the first extensive exhibitions of Cézanne's work.

Vollard commissioned portraits of himself from artists whose work he bought – Cézanne, Picasso, Bonnard and others. Renoir's is one of the least accurate, either as a record of the dealer's ugly, bulldog features, or as an evocation of his cunning, quirky personality. Rather, Renoir chose to depict an archetypal connoisseur, very much in the tradition of such collector portraits of the

Italian Renaissance. At the same time, though, the painting evokes the dealer's power over the sensuous image of a woman, held in his hands and in his gaze; his pudgy fingers are startlingly similar to the limbs of the statuette.

The statuette depicted is by Aristide Maillol, *Crouching Woman* of 1900, apparently in its original plaster form. It was around this time that Maillol, at Vollard's request, visited Renoir to execute a portrait bust of him; the inclusion of the piece by Maillol here may refer to this. Moreover, the simplified, monumental classicism that Maillol evolved from the late 1890s on may well be relevant to the development of Renoir's art during these years. In the 1890s he had looked in particular to the Rococo paintings of French eighteenth-century artists, but after 1900 he deliberately adopted a broader treatment and a more monumental type of composition and modelling – a sort of timeless classicism.

This development appears in *Portrait of Ambroise Vollard* in the firmly modelled, rounded treatment of the figure, far more distinctly separated from its surroundings than the figures of *The Theatre Box* (p. 93), and also in his return to grey and black as a means of modelling. Black had still been used in *The Theatre Box*, but in the mid-1870s Renoir largely abandoned it in favour of modelling suggested by the play of colour alone. He re-adopted black in the 1890s, partly as a result of his studies of the techniques of the Old Masters, and thereafter insisted that it was of prime importance in his palette. Here, the comparatively monochrome treatment of the jacket, with only a few coloured nuances on the folds, is set off against the warmth of the flesh modelling and the background. Blue is used very sparingly, at a few points on the tablecloth and in the pottery.   J.H.

Courtauld Collection [P.1932.SC.340]

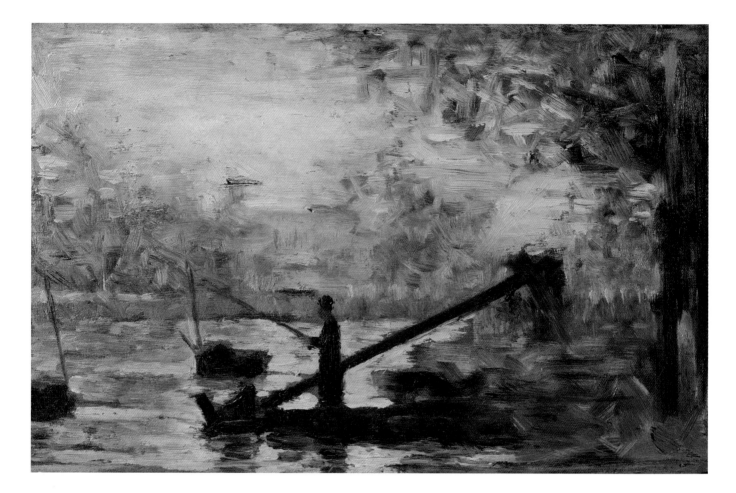

SEURAT, GEORGES 1859–91
Fisherman in a Moored Boat c.1882
Oil on panel, 16.5 x 24.8

Virtually all Seurat's early oil paintings are small studies on wood panels, broadly and seemingly rapidly executed, very probably in front of their outdoor subjects. His preferred subjects, suburban riverside scenes around Paris, were those that the Impressionists favoured, but by the early 1880s such open-air sketching was a common practice, even among artists who, like Seurat, had received a thorough academic training at the Ecole des Beaux-Arts.

Fisherman in a Moored Boat is dominated by the crisp, dark forms of the fisherman,

the boats and the railing, set off against the luminous background – a sharp tonal contrast quite unlike the interplay of clear light colour that the Impressionists used to suggest atmospheric effects. However, deep blues are employed in order to model the dark forms, and soft blues recur in the foliage, which suggests that Seurat was also exploring methods of conveying the atmosphere. These blues are set against the warm orange-brown tones that recur throughout the picture; the latter (again in a way quite unlike Impressionist practice) are primarily obtained, not by applying coloured paint, but by exploiting the rich colour of the underlying unprimed wood panel, the surface of which is wholly

unpainted in places, and elsewhere shows through thinly applied paint layers. In some other small sketches Seurat did adopt the Impressionist practice of painting on a white or very light-toned priming (see p. 97).

This panel does not relate directly to any larger project, but Seurat's many outdoor studies of the early 1880s must all have contributed to his first monumental figure painting, *Bathing at Asnières* (National Gallery, London). The theme of the riverside fisherman was to appear again in the preparatory studies for *A Sunday Afternoon on the Ile de la Grande Jatte* (1884–6).   J.H.

Private Collection, on extended loan to the Courtauld Gallery

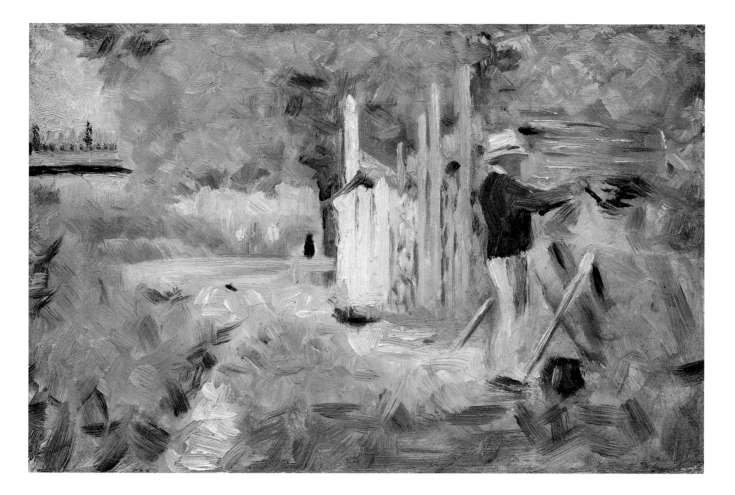

SEURAT, GEORGES 1859–91
Man Painting his Boat c.1883
Oil on panel, 15.9 x 25

The varied palette and strong blue shadows
in this richly coloured painting clearly testify
to the influence of Impressionism. The
work's luminosity is enhanced by the fact
that (unlike most of Seurat's small panel
paintings) the paint was applied over a
white priming, not directly on the wood
panel; although this priming is largely
covered, it is visible just below the feet of
the figure.

The treatment, though, owes little to
Impressionism. The brushwork is relatively
even, built up of crisp little strokes, mainly
applied with quite a wide brush and running
in various directions; the result is an opaque
paint surface of an even rhythm and density.
Only the fence posts, which create a clear-
cut central axis, are treated with longer, more
separated strokes; the man and his boat are
absorbed into the play of deft criss-crossing
touches which fills the rest of the picture.

Man Painting his Boat does not relate to
any larger painting, though it treats a theme
of outdoor recreation by the river, like

Seurat's first major figure painting, *Bathing
at Asnières* (National Gallery, London), on
which the artist was working at this date.
The forms in *Man Painting his Boat* are
treated broadly, without any precise detail,
but in terms of its brushwork, carefully
harmonized throughout the picture, this is
one of the more highly finished of Seurat's
small oils. There is no evidence that he ever
exhibited this panel, but on occasion he did
show such small pictures alongside fully
finished, larger canvases.   J.H.

Courtauld Collection [P.1948.SC.393]

SEURAT, GEORGES 1859–91
The Bridge at Courbevoie c.1886–7
Oil on canvas, 46.4 x 55.3
Signed, bottom left: 'Seurat'

The Bridge at Courbevoie is one of the clearest pictorial manifestos for the divisionist painting technique evolved by Seurat and his colleagues in 1885–6. The technique was intended as a means of translating into paint the effects of natural light and colour, lending a scientific precision to the more empirical solutions that had been adopted by Monet and Pissarro (e.g. *Quays at Rouen*, p. 84). The dot, or point, of colour was the means that seemed best able to control precisely the relative quantities of each colour used in any area of the picture. Although Seurat, like many of his contemporaries, stated that such dots were intended to produce an 'optical mixture' of colour, this is not exactly what takes place, for the dots are not small enough to fuse and produce a single colour when seen from a normal viewing distance. Pissarro, at the time that he was closely associated with Seurat, stated that the optimum viewing distance was three times the diagonal measurement of any picture – which in this case would mean a little over 2 metres or 7 feet. The effect of the canvas from this distance is that the dots are still clearly visible as dots, and the colours can still be identified separately; far from fusing, they seem to shimmer and vibrate – in a sense to recreate something of the impression of vibration produced by outdoor sunlight, but recreated by the complex artifice of painting technique. Ogden Rood's *Modern Chromatics* (1879; French translation 1881), one of the manuals of colour theory that Seurat studied most carefully, noted this phenomenon, quoting the findings of the German physicist Dove,

and it seems certain that Seurat was deliberately seeking such effects.

Here, Seurat's analysis of the different elements present in a light effect is most evident in the treatment of the river bank. The dominant colour is green (the 'local' colour of grass), rather lighter and yellower in the sunlight, duller and bluer in shadow; warm, pinker touches further enliven the sunlit grass, and clear blues the shadowed areas. In addition, there is a scattering of mauve touches across most of the shadowed grass, and they reappear in the topmost band of sunlit grass, along the edge of the river. The scientific justification for these is unclear: they may be meant to suggest a complementary colour induced by the green of the grass, or simply to evoke the warmth of the light of the sun; their effect is to enhance the play of warm and cool colours, which gives the surface its richness and mobility. The background is treated with softer, paler hues, the same colour being repeated in many parts of the picture, in a way closely comparable to the background of Pissarro's *Quays at Rouen*.

The scene represents the Ile de la Grande Jatte in the river Seine, looking south-west, upstream towards the bridge. The same stretch of river bank is seen in the opposite direction in *A Sunday Afternoon on the Ile de la Grande Jatte*, but in contrast to the elaborate parade of modern society seen there, *The Bridge at Courbevoie* is still and silent, with three small figures standing motionless by the river. The mood is difficult to interpret; although the work has recently been described as a 'plangent evocation of melancholy and alienation', Seurat employs none of the devices then favoured by French painters to evoke these feelings – indeed, he seems to have studiously avoided any clear indication of its mood. However, the picture retains

an intriguing strangeness through its very stillness, and through the curious juxtaposition of the foliated trees on the left, and the bare branches on the right (traces of overpainted foliage can still be seen to the left of this tree). All the elements are presented in an ordered, harmonious co-existence; the vertical of the central factory chimney is closely paralleled by the boats' masts and the fence-posts, establishing with the figures a taut series of pictorial intervals.

There is a further oddity: the vertical elements – the chimney, the masts and the house on the far right – are all at a slight but perceptible angle. Seurat organized his compositions with such care that this cannot be accidental; the effect is to emphasize the parallel lines within the picture, for the viewer's eye does not immediately relate them to the grid of the frame.

A number of adjustments and alterations are visible; their presence tends to underline the care that Seurat took over the placing of the compositional elements. For example, the foliage on the trees on the left has been reduced and the tall mast immediately adjacent partially painted out. Over and above these changes, the canvas was clearly the result of an elaborate reworking, with small dots of colour added over broader paint layers. A detailed preparatory drawing exists for the whole composition. Moreover, the play of shadow in the foreground is so specific, and (if it records an actual effect) must have changed so rapidly that Seurat would have had little opportunity to capture it on the spot. Later, he came to use his pointillist technique to achieve far more overtly artificial effects (see *Young Woman Powdering Herself*, p. 101), though he continued to use it for landscape scenes. J.H.

Courtauld Collection [P.1948.SC.394]

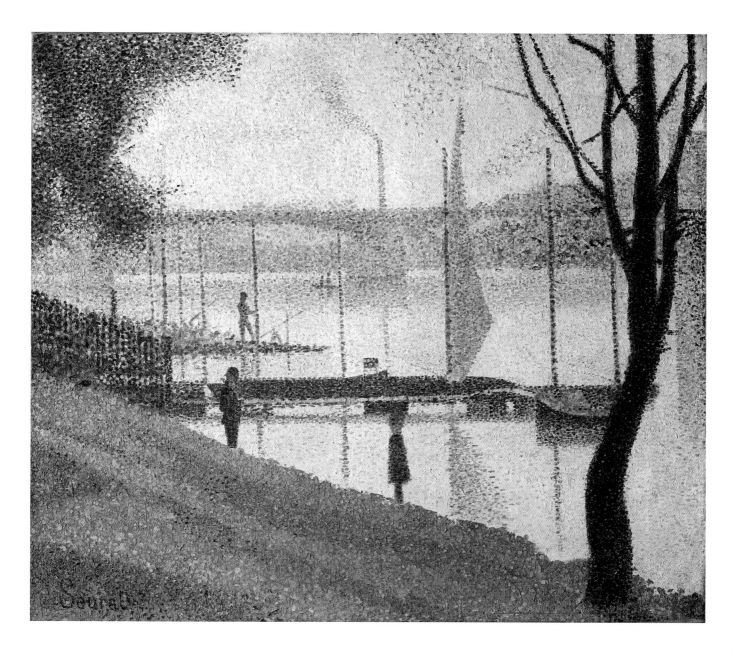

SEURAT, GEORGES 1859–91
Young Woman Powdering Herself c.1888–90
Oil on canvas, 95.5 x 79.5
Signed, on painted border, bottom right:
'Seurat'

This is the only one of Seurat's paintings which reflects anything about his private existence; it shows his mistress, Madeleine Knobloch, at her toilette, though the identity of the model was not revealed in the catalogue of the Indépendants exhibition of 1890, where the canvas was first shown. Apparently Seurat's own face originally appeared in the frame on the wall, but a friend warned him that this might appear laughable and he replaced it with the vase of flowers. Examination of the painting shows that the artist did obliterate a previous reflection in the mirror, but the indications cannot confidently be identified as the face of Seurat himself.

The painting is composed of a sequence of contrasts and visual incongruities – between the massive figure and her impracticably small table, and between the rounded forms in the foreground and the angularity of the picture frame and the wall decoration.

Seurat left no indication of the picture's meaning, but the work contains many examples of his sign for happiness and gaiety: the motif of lines rising from a point, which is used here to decorate the wall. This motif is echoed in many other parts of the picture, and even by the curl of hair behind the model's neck. But Seurat does not seem to have been using these directional lines in a literal way to uplift the spirits of the viewer. They all belong to the woman's personal décor, to her furniture and cosmetics; the weighty model and her impassive expression counteract them, and the spirit which emerges from the painting is more ironic than lighthearted.

In this light, the picture explores a theme that was recurrent in Seurat's art – the contrast between nature and artifice; the art of cosmetics, like the model's corsetry, force nature into the mould of fashion. The spectator catches her in the process of rendering her natural self artificial. The satire is not, though, directed against the model herself, but rather against her trappings, which were so characteristic a part of urban life; in these terms, the theme explores the anomalous relationships that

existed between public and private life in contemporary Paris.

The brushwork and colours are used to augment the pictorial impact of the canvas. The background wall becomes darker and bluer where it approaches the lit contours of the figure, and lighter where it meets its shadowed edges; throughout the picture there is an eddy of interwoven warm and cool touches, creating a shimmering effect over the whole surface, but without suggesting closely observed lighting. This effect is augmented by the way in which the painted border changes in colour so as to achieve maximum contrast with the area of the picture next to it. The arched top of this border seems to make the picture itself into a sort of altarpiece or shrine – like the little table and mirror before which the model sits. The dots of colour, though comparatively even in size, are often slightly elongated and follow the contours of the forms; this final 'skin' of colour was added gradually over more broadly applied layers of paint, as Seurat worked up the picture to completion.   J.H.

Courtauld Collection [P.1932.SC.396]

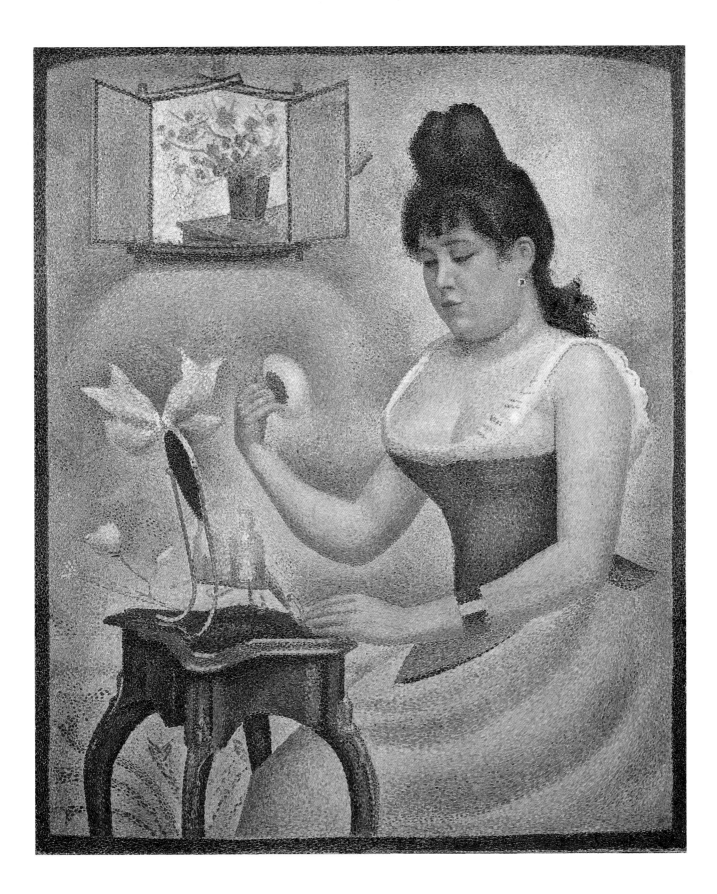

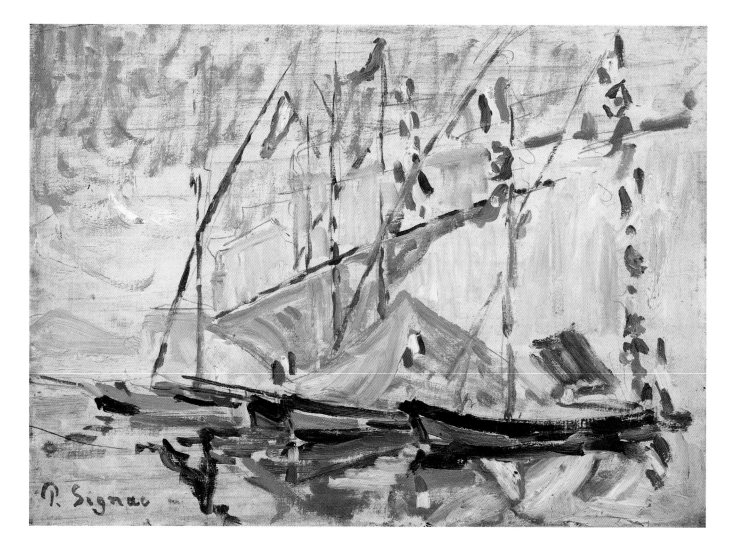

SIGNAC, PAUL 1863–1935
Saint-Tropez c.1893
Oil on panel, 19.5 x 28
Signed, bottom left: 'P. Signac', and on
reverse: 'P.S. St Tropez'

Saint-Tropez is a preparatory study for *The
Port of Saint-Tropez,* dated 1893 (Van der
Heydt-Museum, Wuppertal), which shows
just the same arrangement, but is presented
in a vertical format, including a wider zone
of reflections in the water at the base. The
finished painting is handled in the rather
larger and bolder version of the pointillist
brushwork that Signac evolved after Seurat's
death in 1891.

During the 1890s, Signac began to execute
his finished paintings entirely in the studio,
working out of doors in front of the subject
only on small studies in oil or watercolour.

However, it is not clear whether the present
picture is one of these open-air studies. It
includes extensive fluent underdrawing that
closely conforms to the final forms of the
larger painting; moreover, the paint
handling, very varied and rather schematic,
is quite unlike that of the rapidly brushed
sketches of natural subjects that Signac was
producing in these years. It seems more
likely that *Saint-Tropez* served as a sort of
cartoon for the final painting, notating in
summary form both its compositional
arrangement and the essentials of its colour
composition – the arcs of masts and sails
played off against the houses, and the blues
of the sky and central sail set against the
yellow and orange of the sunlit buildings.

Painted the year after Signac moved to
Saint-Tropez, then a remote and little-
known fishing village on the Mediterranean

coast, this canvas illustrates the intense
colour contrasts that Signac evolved during
the early to mid-1890s in order to capture
the effect of bright Mediterranean light
(compare Monet, *Antibes,* p. 89). The
luminosity of the white-primed wood panel
enhances the effect.

Signac regularly included oil studies and
watercolours in his exhibitions, alongside
finished paintings, indicating that he
regarded his studies as works of art in their
own right, and not merely as preparatory
material. The bold and improvisatory
application of vivid colour in his sketches
had a significant influence on the Fauve style
evolved by Matisse and Derain in 1905 –
Matisse worked with Signac at Saint-Tropez
in 1904. J.H.

Courtauld Collection [P.1948.SC.408]

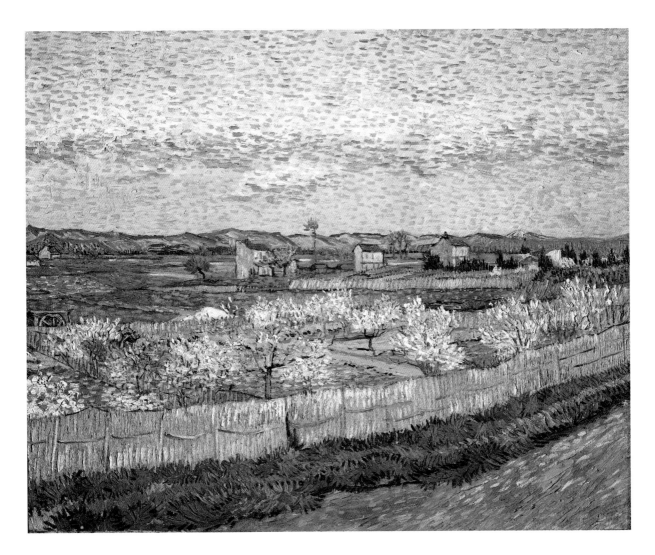

GOGH, VINCENT VAN   1853–90
The Crau at Arles: Peach Trees in Flower
1889
Oil on canvas, 65 x 81

Painted in Arles in spring 1889, this canvas shows a partial view of the Crau (the wide plain to the east of Arles and the river Rhône) looking towards the Alpilles – the range of hills seen in the background. Van Gogh sent a rough pen-and-ink sketch of the composition to Paul Signac, and described the picture:

> I have just come back with two studies of orchards. Here is a crude sketch of them – the big one is a poor landscape with little cottages, blue skyline of the Alpille foothills, sky white and blue. The foreground, patches of land surrounded by cane hedges, where small peach trees are in blossom – everything is small there, the gardens, the fields, the orchards and the trees, even the mountains, as in certain Japanese landscapes, which is the reason why the subject attracted me.

The idea of the south of France as a Western equivalent of Japan had been one of van Gogh's main reasons for travelling to Arles the previous year; here, the seemingly snowcapped peak in the right background may be an echo of Mount Fuji-Yama.

The Crau at Arles: Peach Trees in Flower was painted after Gauguin's visit to Arles, during which he had advised van Gogh to work from his imagination; it marks van Gogh's renewed commitment to painting from nature. In contrast to Gauguin's schematic paint surfaces (see p. 105), van Gogh conveys the complex textures and patterns of the chosen scene with a great variety of brush-marks, some broad and incisive, but others of extreme finesse. The laden dabs of paint in the blossom reflect his study of Impressionist painting in Paris, but elsewhere the forms are far crisper and more clearly drawn, particularly in the very fine, dark-red strokes added in many parts of the picture at a very late stage in its execution in order to emphasize the forms of the

elements shown – in the houses, the trees and the foreground verge. Added very late, too, was the sequence of blue strokes on the road at the bottom, together with blue accents elsewhere in the landscape and sky; these knit the main elements of the scene together into an atmospheric unity.

Despite its visible debts to Impressionism, the picture's subject also reflects van Gogh's Dutch heritage. He often likened the wide spaces of the Crau to the panoramas of Dutch seventeenth-century landscape painting. In 1888, he had written: 'Here, except for an intenser colouring, it reminds one of Holland: everything is flat, only one thinks of the Holland of Ruysdael or Hobbema or Ostade rather than of Holland as it is.' By including the working figure on the left, along with the prominent small houses, van Gogh emphasized that this was a social, agricultural landscape, its forms the result of man's intervention.   J.H.

Courtauld Collection [P.1932.SC.176]

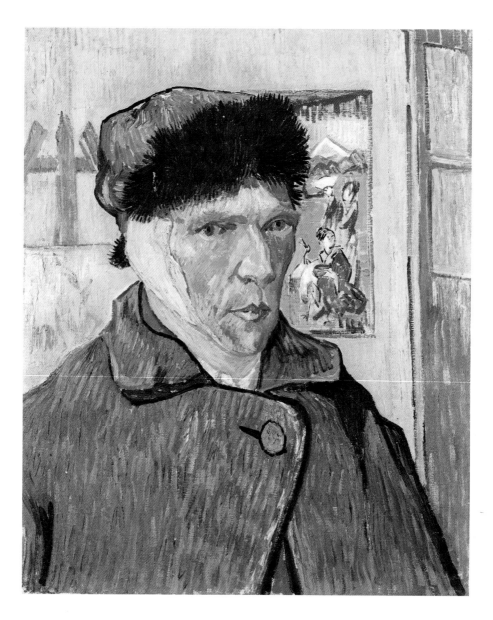

GOGH, VINCENT VAN 1853–90
Self-Portrait with Bandaged Ear 1889
Oil on canvas, 60 x 49

On 24 December 1888, van Gogh mutilated his ear after a quarrel with Paul Gauguin, who had spent the previous two months staying with van Gogh in Arles. This radical act and Gauguin's departure marked the end of van Gogh's dreams of setting up a 'studio of the South' for like-minded artists. The present work and another self-portrait (Private Collection, USA) seem to have been two of the first pictures van Gogh painted after leaving hospital around 6 January 1889.

Van Gogh's differences with Gauguin were grounded on a fundamental aesthetic issue – whether a painter should work from nature or from the imagination. For Gauguin, reliance on external appearances marked a lack of creative power, while van Gogh found rich layers of meaning in the natural world. During Gauguin's stay, he painted a few canvases from the imagination, but a year later, he wrote to the painter Emile Bernard, 'Once or twice, . . . I gave myself free rein with abstractions and at that time abstraction seemed to be a charming path. But it is enchanted ground, and one soon finds oneself up against a stone wall.'

Self-Portrait with Bandaged Ear marks van Gogh's reversion to an aesthetic grounded in nature. The painter translates his own appearance into varied and improvisatory rhythms of touch and colour, in marked contrast to the simplified, schematic surfaces that Gauguin advocated. The paint-handling distinguishes the textures of the different elements in the figure; a swathe of white suggests the bandage, while the flesh of the face is indicated in a network of nuanced coloured touches and crowned by the crisp strokes of the brim of the cap. The face includes a remarkable diversity of colours, with those on the cheek alone ranging from mauve and pink to orange, yellow and green. The intense green of the eyes is set against the startling red that marks out the eyelids.

The imagery is evidently related to the recent events. The bandaged ear is given great prominence, and on each side of the head we see a highly loaded image; to the left, an easel with a scarcely worked canvas on it; to the right, a Japanese colour print by Torakiyo that van Gogh owned (in order to fit it alongside his face, van Gogh adapted it, moving the figures over to its right edge). The print is a very typical image of the mid-nineteenth century, showing an idyllic view of Japan as a land of beautiful women and landscape.   J.H.

Courtauld Collection [P.1949.SC.175]

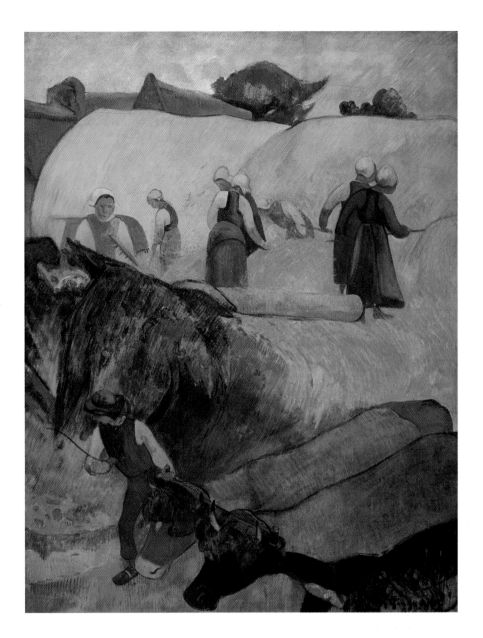

GAUGUIN, PAUL 1848–1903
The Haystacks 1889
Oil on canvas, 92 x 73.3
Signed, bottom right: 'P. Gauguin '89'

This haymaking scene was painted at
Pont-Aven in Brittany in July 1889. Gauguin
had first visited Pont-Aven in 1886, partly to
get away from Paris, and partly to find a
cheaper place to live. Brittany was by then
becoming an attractive tourist centre, and
was gaining in agricultural prosperity, but it
retained an image as a place where primitive
peasant types and folkloric customs could
still readily be found. Paintings featuring
picturesque Breton costumes and customs
were common among the works shown at
the annual Salon exhibitions in Paris. At
Pont-Aven – one of the main artists' colonies
in Brittany – a group of younger painters

formed around Gauguin, all of whom shared
his commitment to rejecting the use of
naturalistic depiction in favour of an art
which expressed the primitive essence of
Breton life.

Gauguin had worked with Pissarro in the
late 1870s and early 1880s, and painted at
times in a style very close to his. In the
mid-1880s, though, he began to simplify his
forms, rejecting the variegated textures and
rich surface effects associated with
Impressionism in favour of clearer, more
stylized surface pattern.

In *The Haystacks* the brushwork is quite
thin and crisp, lacking the density and
flexibility of Pissarro's, and a clear dominant
colour is evident in each area. Gauguin had
painted with Cézanne in 1881, and in some
ways his handling here reflects Cézanne's
example, particularly in the sequences of

parallel strokes. However, Gauguin's
brushwork is thinner and streakier, his
drawing far more schematic, and there is
little hint of the nuances of atmospheric
colour so prominent in Cézanne's and
Pissarro's work. Moreover, Gauguin
presented the space in his picture in a way
that cannot readily be understood. The
forms seem to be stacked one on top of the
other; the fine diagonal strokes above the
necks of the oxen wholly ignore the spatial
recession which is suggested below and to
the right of the bush.

The simplified forms of the oxen and the
rhythmic poses of the Breton women evoke
a sense of timeless rural labour, presenting
the activities depicted as if they were a sort
of secular ritual.   J.H.

Courtauld Collection [P.1932.SC.162]

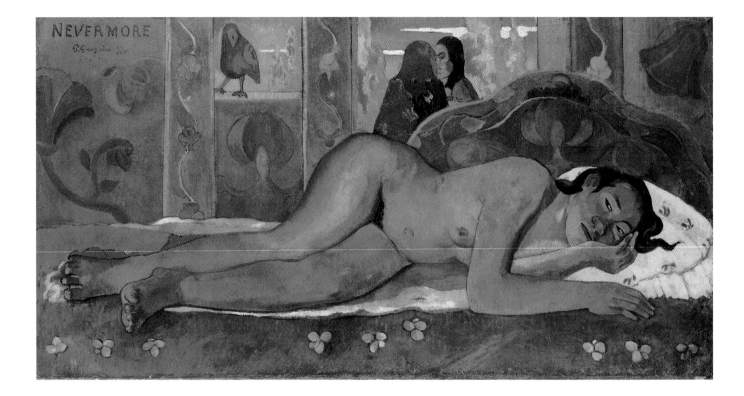

GAUGUIN, PAUL 1848–1903
Nevermore 1897
Oil on canvas, 60.5 x 116
Signed, top left: 'NEVERMORE /
P. Gauguin 97 / O. TAITI'

Gauguin painted *Nevermore* in February 1897, during his second visit to Tahiti. He described the painting in a letter addressed to Daniel de Monfreid, who acted as his agent in Paris:

> I wished to suggest by means of a simple nude a certain long-lost barbarian luxury. The whole is drowned in colours which are deliberately sombre and sad . . . Man's imagination alone has enriched the dwelling with his fantasy. As a title, Nevermore; not the raven of Edgar Poe, but the bird of the devil that is keeping watch. It is badly painted . . . but no matter, I think it's a good canvas.

Nevermore belongs to a long tradition of reclining female nudes, echoing the sensuous exoticism of painters like Ingres; but here Gauguin reworked the tradition, producing a complex and challenging image. There is a triangular relationship between the nude figure, the bird, seemingly watching, and the clothed figures beyond, turned away and talking. The nude's eyes suggest that she is aware of the bird or the other figures, but otherwise nothing is clear. The contrasts of unclothed with clothed, of reverie with conversation, evoke the loss of innocence; Gauguin's reference to a 'certain long-lost barbarian luxury' seems to suggest that the image relates not only to the awakening of a particular woman, but also to the corruption of 'primitive' cultures by the influx of Western values.

The bird's role, too, is ambiguous. Though Gauguin denied its relationship to Poe's *The Raven*, the bird, along with the title inscribed on the picture, would inevitably have evoked Poe's poem for the painting's viewers. Gauguin may have wanted to avoid too explicit a literary reference, but the bird's presence here is as ominous as it is in the poem, in which it stands above the poet's door, croaking 'Nevermore'. In the picture it contributes to the sense of threat invading the luxury of the nude's surroundings.

The lavish decoration of the interior, as Gauguin's letter insists, is imaginary. The stylized gourds on the bed-head and beneath the bird hint at sexual penetration, relating the décor more closely with the figures, but without any precise meaning. Allusive elements like these were central to Gauguin's idea of Symbolism.

The effect of *Nevermore* is heightened by its surface and colour. The sharp yellow of the nude's pillow and the red by her feet heighten her strangeness and further separate her from her surroundings. The smooth, dense surface (quite unlike *Te Rerioa*, shown opposite) enhances this effect, although it was created purely for practical reasons: *Nevermore* was painted over another subject, which was covered with a further layer of white priming before Gauguin resumed work on the canvas. However, the final effect makes positive use of the density of these underlying layers; clearly Gauguin found that they gave the picture a distinctive physical quality.   J.H.

Courtauld Collection [P.1932.SC.163]

106

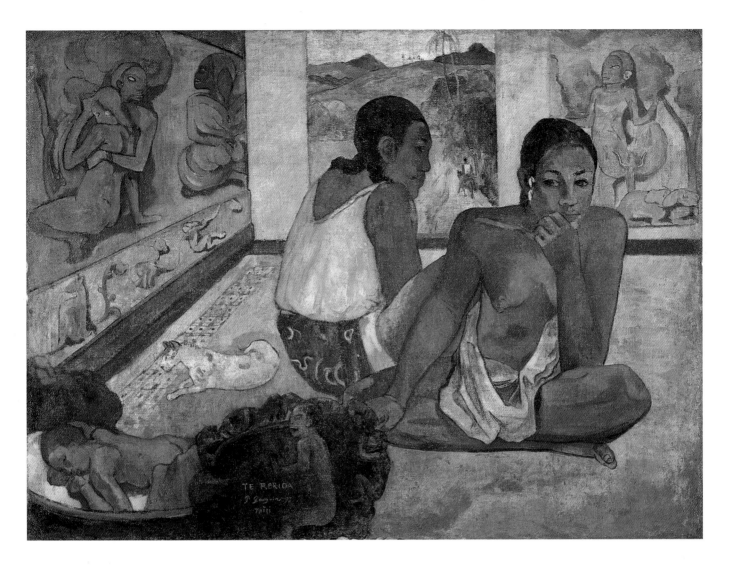

GAUGUIN, PAUL 1848–1903
Te Rerioa (The Dream) 1897
Oil on canvas, 95.1 x 130.2
Signed, bottom left centre: 'TE RERIOA /
P. Gauguin 97 / TAITI'

Te Rerioa was painted in Tahiti in March
1897, about three weeks after *Nevermore*.
The decorations on the walls seem to have
been largely imaginary, created to serve as
appropriate décor for the picture; the animal
on the far left in the decoration is the only
kangaroo in Post-Impressionist painting.
The carvings on the cradle relate to a carved
bowl by the Maori carver Patoromu
Tamatea, probably made in the 1860s, which
Gauguin had seen in the Auckland Museum
in 1895.

Gauguin used these words to describe the
painting in a letter when he despatched it to
Daniel de Monfreid in France:

Te Rereioa (the Dream), that is the title.
Everything is dream in this canvas; is it the
child? is it the mother? is it the horseman on
the path? or even is it the dream of the
painter!!! All that is incidental to painting,
some will say. Who knows. Maybe it isn't.

The spelling of the Tahitian title in this letter
is correct; it is wrongly spelt on the canvas.
The word in fact means 'nightmare', but, as
he wrote, Gauguin was using it more
generally to mean 'dream'.

The uncertainties which Gauguin spelt
out in this playful fashion are integral to
the painting, since none of the figures
communicate with each other, and none has
a clearly legible expression. The image as a
whole is made up from a set of contrasts:
sleeping child and daydreaming women;
sleeping child and the seemingly active,
carved figure on the cradle; the two seated
women in a state of repose and the figures
making love in the wall decoration; the
principal figures seated passively and the
active man, riding on the path and seen
between the heads of the two women; the
live animal on the floor beside carved
animals on the wall decoration.

Gauguin's letter insists that none of the
elements in the picture is 'real'; this is
emphasized by the physical appearance of
the painting itself – thinly and broadly
painted over coarse sacking, so that its
flatness and the physical presence of the
paint and the sacking are clearly apparent.

Te Rerioa was intended for a European
audience, presenting an archetype of
'primitive' reverie in unspoilt surroundings,
and a fusion of eroticism and innocence.
This vision bore no relation to the state of
society in Tahiti in the 1890s, but the picture
belonged to a long European tradition of
images of the 'noble savage'. These visions
owe their origins not to the 'primitive'
worlds they show, but to the reactions of
Europeans against modern urban life in the
West; the idyllic images that they present of
the 'otherness' of their subjects belong firmly
in the West, as projections of dissatisfaction
with the values of Western society.   J.H.

Courtauld Collection [P.1932.SC.164]

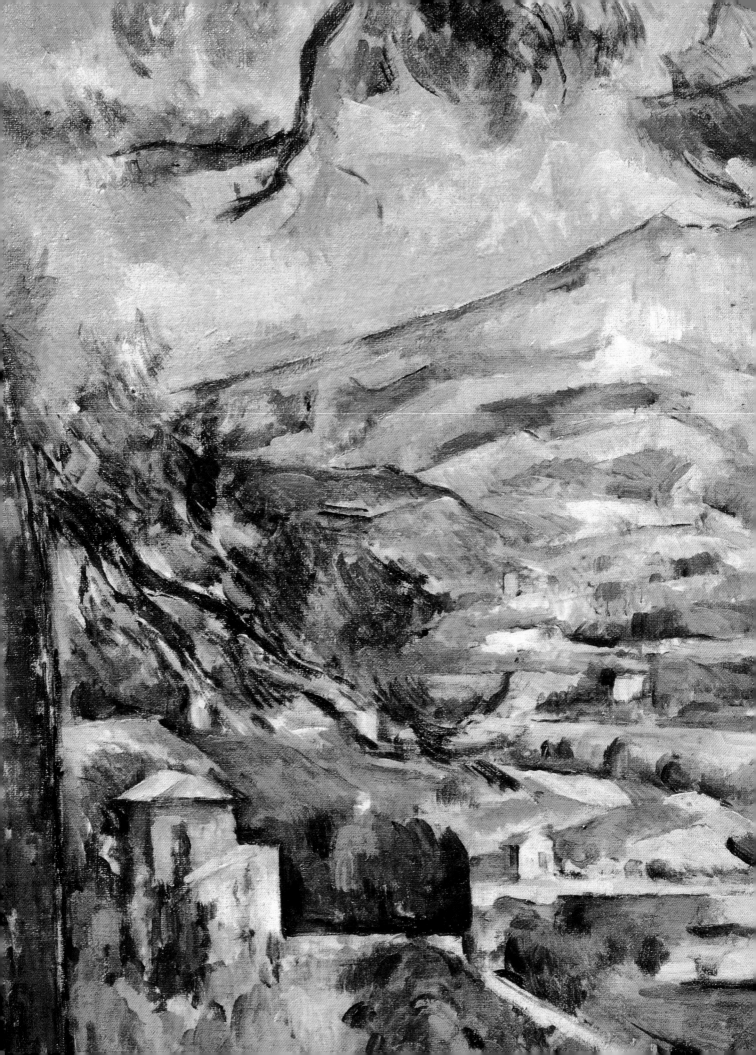

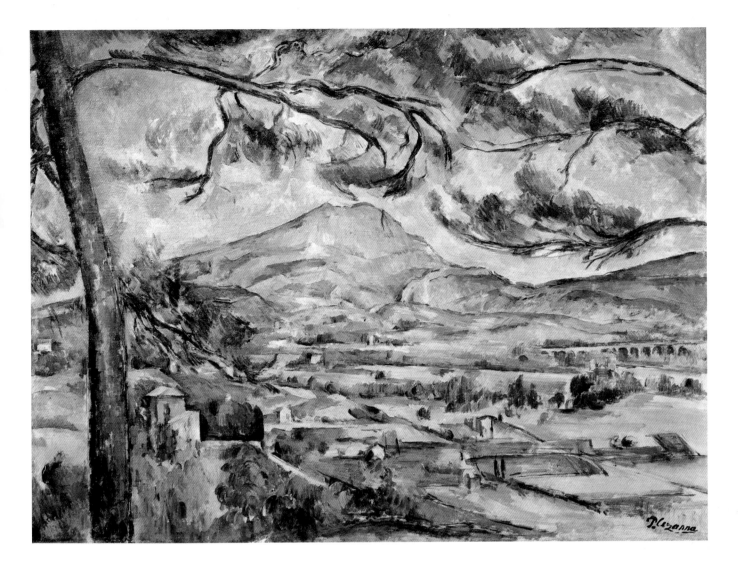

CÉZANNE, PAUL 1839–1906
The Montagne Sainte-Victoire c.1887
Oil on canvas, 66.8 x 92.3
Signed, bottom right: 'P. Cézanne'

The Montagne Sainte-Victoire is situated
to the east of Cézanne's birthplace,
Aix-en-Provence, and its broken silhouette
dominates the town. Cézanne painted it
throughout his career, and it was a subject to
which he attributed great significance. Here,
it is seen from a point to the west of Aix,
near Cézanne's family home, the Jas de
Bouffan, with the valley of the river Arc in
the foreground.

In reality, the mountain peak lies about
8 miles (13 km) away, but here Cézanne, by
focusing on a comparatively small part of the
scene in front of him, gave the mountain the
dominant role in the composition. We now
tend to see this scene as unspoiled and even
timeless, but the presence of the prominent
railway viaduct at the far right would have

been a strongly contemporary reference for
the picture's original viewers.

When this painting was shown at the
exhibition of the Société des Amis des Arts
at Aix (a society of amateur artists) in 1895,
it attracted the admiration of the young poet
Joachim Gasquet, son of a childhood friend
of Cézanne. When Cézanne realized that
Gasquet's praise was sincere, he signed the
picture and presented it to him. This
landscape is thus one of the very few
paintings dating from after 1880 to which
Cézanne added his signature.

The picture shows a simplification of
Cézanne's technique. Traces of the system of
parallel brush-strokes that he had used
c.1880 remain, but most of the paint areas
are flatter and less variegated, with soft
nuances of colour introduced to suggest
surface texture and the play of light. In
places the cream priming of the canvas is left
bare (see detail), and its luminosity
contributes to the overall tonality of the

picture. Traces of the initial underdrawing,
in Prussian blue paint, remain visible in the
final state of the painting.

Recession into distance is suggested by
colour and line. There is a gradual transition
from the foreground's clearer greens and
orange-yellows to the softer blues and pinks
on the mountain, but even the foreground
foliage is tinged with blue; pinks and reds –
notably on the branch silhouetted against
the sky – serve to knit the foreground forms
to the far mountain. Alongside this, a
network of quite linear contours, suggesting
fences, walls and the edges of fields, leads the
eye into the distance. The placing of the
overhanging branches, carefully framing the
contour of the mountain, enhances this
surface coherence. The treatment of the
picture as a whole transforms the natural
subject into a composition of great order
and monumentality.   J.H.

Courtauld Collection [P.1934.SC.55]

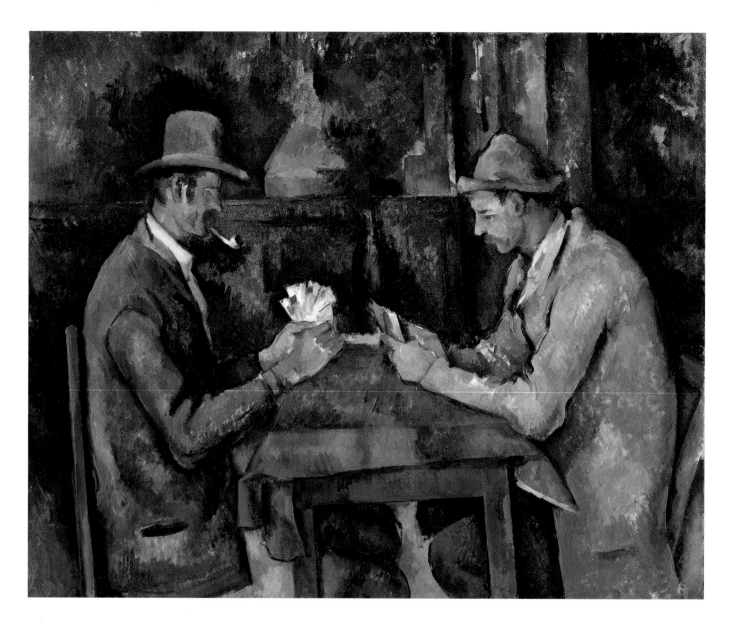

CÉZANNE, PAUL 1839–1906
The Card Players c.1892–5
Oil on canvas, 60 x 73

During the 1890s Cézanne painted a
sequence of canvases of groups of men
playing cards. Two show three players, with
spectators (Metropolitan Museum of Art,
New York, and Barnes Foundation, Merion,
Pa.), and were probably painted first; in the
other three the subject is simplified, with
two men facing each other, seen in profile
as here.

The tonality of the present picture is quite
subdued, but a wide range of colour is used
to model the figures and their surroundings,
with soft atmospheric blues set against the
warm hues on the tablecloth and elsewhere.
The colour is simply brushed on to the
canvas for the most part, but at certain
points, notably in the men's faces, delicate

crisper accents suggest their modelling more
closely; elsewhere, for instance in the hands,
small zones of unpainted primed canvas
suggest the play of light.

There are certain clear divergences from
'normal' vision: the verticals of the table lean
to the left, and the knees of the left figure
extend unduly far to the right. Such oddities
were not wilful and deliberate distortions;
rather, they emerged during the execution of
the painting, as Cézanne focused on
relationships of colour and tone, rather than
literal representation of the subject. When
friends pointed out the oddities in his
canvases, he used to laugh them off: 'I am a
primitive, I've got a lazy eye,' he told two
young artists in 1905.

Cézanne was also much concerned with
his subject matter. In the *Card Players*
paintings he looked to a long tradition of
images of figures seated around tables,

perhaps in particular to the art of the
seventeenth-century Le Nain brothers. At
the same time he worked closely from direct
observation, using local peasants as models.
Cézanne felt that peasant life enshrined
traditional values, which he saw as being
threatened by urban fashions; late in life, he
told Jules Borély:

> Today everything has changed in reality, but
> not for me, I live in the town of my childhood,
> and it is with the eyes of the people of my own
> age that I see again the past. I love above all else
> the appearance of people who have grown old
> without breaking with old customs.

In this sense, the image of peasants
concentrating on their game of cards is the
living counterpart to the landscape of the
Montagne Sainte-Victoire (see p. 109) that
held such significance for him.   J.H.

Courtauld Collection [P.1932.SC.57]

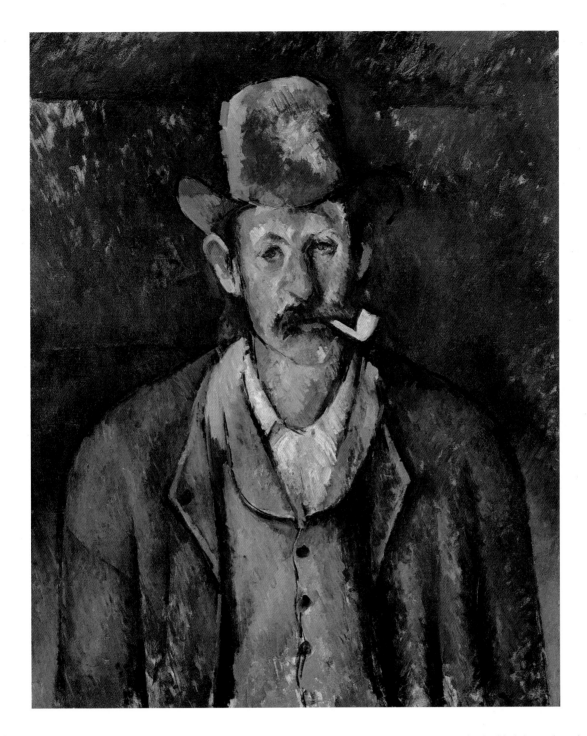

CÉZANNE, PAUL 1839–1906
Man with a Pipe c.1892–5
Oil on canvas, 73 x 60

The model is the same as that for the left-hand figure in *The Card Players* (opposite); he was a peasant gardener, apparently named *le père* Alexandre. The two paintings were probably executed at much the same date, since they are very similar in colour and handling. Here the man's face, which provides the prime focus of the composition, is more elaborated than any part of *The Card Players*: areas of the face are treated with successions of diagonal strokes, reminiscent of the type of brush-stroke that Cézanne had employed a decade earlier.

The face is modelled by the contrast between the dull blues in the shadows and rich warm hues in the lit areas; this contrast is heightened by two particularly crisp, bold strokes of red added down the ridge of the nose at a very late stage in the execution of the painting, set against the deep blues alongside them.

As in *The Card Players,* the simple, monumental form of the figure is used to suggest the timeless, traditional values which Cézanne attributed to the old peasants of the Aix region.   J.H.

Courtauld Collection [P.1932.SC.58]

CÉZANNE, PAUL 1839–1906
Still Life with Plaster Cast c.1894
Oil on paper, laid on board 70.6 x 57.3

Cézanne's still lifes perhaps reveal his changing preoccupations most fully, since still life gave him the freedom to choose and arrange the combination of objects he wanted to depict. A witness described the complex business of setting up one such still-life subject:

> The cloth was arranged on the table, with innate taste. Then Cézanne arranged the fruits, contrasting the tones one against the other, making the complementaries vibrate, the greens against the reds, the yellows against the blues, tipping, turning, balancing the fruit as he wanted them to be, using coins of one or two sous for the purpose. He brought to this task the greatest care and many precautions; one guessed it was to him a feast for the eye.

Still Life with Plaster Cast is one of the most complex of his late still lifes, both in its composition and through the inclusion of the cast and other works of art. The plaster cast of a Cupid (formerly attributed to Pierre Puget) still remains in Cézanne's studio at Aix, as does the cast of a flayed man which is

seen in the painting at the top of the present picture. The Cupid cast is in reality 18 inches (46 cm) high, and it appears larger than life in the painting. The same is true of the canvas that is shown learning again the wall on the left, *Still Life with Peppermint Bottle* (National Gallery of Art, Washington DC), which was painted at much the same time as this picture; the area of it that we see, which includes the red stripe and blue area at top left, is shown here larger than it is in the original canvas, although implicitly it is standing on the floor well beyond the foreground table. The far apple, apparently placed on the distant floor, appears as large as the fruit on the table.

There are ambiguities, too, in the relationships between the objects. The 'real' blue drapery at the bottom left merges with the painted still life in the pictures on the left; the foliage of the 'real' onion fuses with the table-leg in the same still life; and the back edge of the table-top virtually dissolves into the floor to the left of this onion. There is also genuine uncertainty about the arrangement of planes in the background, where the edges of the canvas depicting the flayed figure cannot be clearly determined.

The inconsistencies and paradoxes of the space are compounded by the paradoxes about the nature of the reality depicted which recur throughout the picture: between 'real' and painted fruit and drapery; between 'real' fruit on the table and the Cupid figure – a cast of a statue; and between this cast and the flayed man beyond – a painting of a cast of a statue. All of these devices seem to stress the artificiality of the picture itself – of its grouping and of its making; of all Cézanne's still lifes, this one reveals most vividly the artificiality of the idea of *nature morte*, an assemblage of objects, arranged in order to be painted, and, beyond this, the artifice of the art of painting itself.

Some sketching, probably in pencil, is clearly seen in normal light as underdrawing for the apples, and infra-red photography has revealed more underdrawing in the Cupid's face. There are other areas where no underdrawing is visible and the image is started and finished in paint. In one area, the apple on the lower edge, there is pencil drawing on top of the paint. J.H.

Courtauld Collection [P.1948.SC.59]

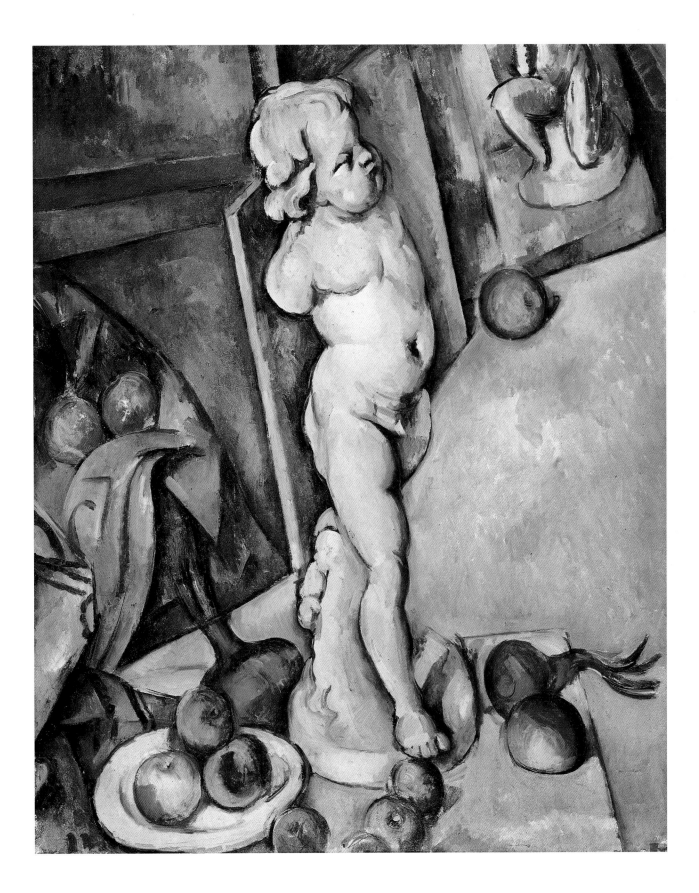

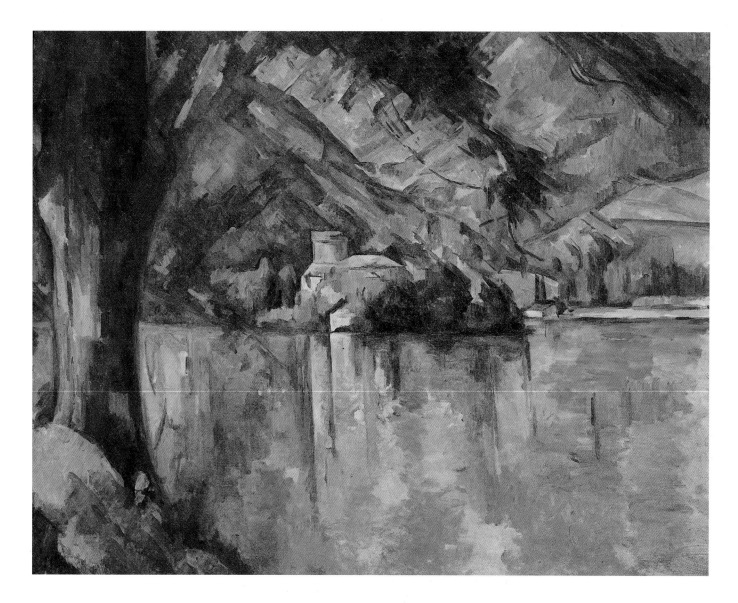

CÉZANNE, PAUL 1839–1906
The Lac d'Annecy 1896
Oil on canvas, 65 x 81

The Lac d'Annecy was painted in July 1896
at Talloires on the shores of this lake in
Haute-Savoie, in the foothills of the French
Alps, looking towards the Château de
Duingt, half-hidden by trees on the far side
of the lake. Cézanne wrote in a letter to
Gasquet from Talloires:

This is a temperate zone. The surrounding hills
are quite lofty. The lake, which at this point
narrows to a bottleneck, seems to lend itself to
the line drawing exercises of young ladies.
Certainly it is still a bit of nature, but a little
like we've been taught to see it in the albums of
young lady travellers.

In this canvas, with its vibrant colour and
monumental structure, Cézanne was clearly
determined to transcend this commonplace
picturesque.

The painting as a whole is dominated by
a cool colour range of blues and greens,
sometimes deep and sonorous in tone, but
its principal focuses are provided by the
succession of warm accents which runs
across it: the areas where the early morning
sunshine strikes the tree-trunk on the left,
the distant hills and the buildings on the
opposite shore.

The composition is carefully structured,
with the massive bulk of the tree as a
repoussoir on the left and its branches
enclosing the top (see *The Montagne
Sainte-Victoire*, p. 109); the scene is anchored
in the centre by the tighter, rectilinear forms
of the buildings and their elongated
reflections. In reality, the castle is about a
mile (1.6 km) away across the water from
Cézanne's viewpoint, but, by focusing
closely on it, he made it seem closer. The
reflections are slightly distorted – like the
table-legs in *The Card Players* (see p. 110)

they are not exactly vertical; Cézanne would
often ignore discrepancies of this sort as he
concentrated on the relationships of colour
and form in his canvases.

The brushwork in the background builds
up a sequence of planes of colour, uniting
the nearby foliage to the far hillsides; but at
certain points cursive, graphic arcs detach
themselves from the foliage, and accentuate
the sense of formal rhythm and pattern
across the top of the canvas. Such devices,
which were employed to give a unified
structure to the whole surface, became an
even more prominent feature of Cézanne's
last works, but this technique was not a
means of rejecting nature; rather he was
seeking, he said, to achieve a 'harmony
parallel to nature'; it was thus that he hoped
to transform his experiences of the visible
world into a lasting, coherent art.   J.H.

Courtauld Collection [P.1932.SC.60]

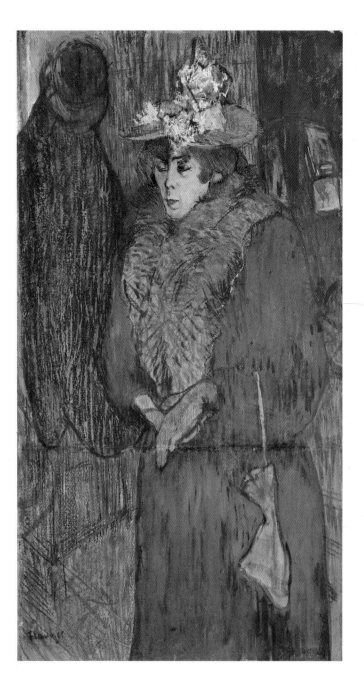

TOULOUSE-LAUTREC, HENRI DE
1864–1901
Jane Avril in the Entrance of the Moulin Rouge, putting on her Gloves 1892
Pastel and oil on millboard, laid on panel, 102 x 55.1
Signed, bottom left, initials in monogram: 'T-Lautrec'

Jane Avril was a celebrated popular dancer, who first appeared at the Moulin Rouge in 1889, and became one of its star performers. She was nicknamed La Mélinite (the name of a recently invented form of explosive). She was one of Lautrec's favourite models, and became his close friend and supporter. The English poet Arthur Symons described

his first experience of watching her dance in 1892: 'Young and girlish, the more provocative because she played as a prude, with an assumed modesty, décolletée nearly to the waist, in the Oriental fashion. She had about her an air of depraved virginity.'

However, Lautrec depicted her here in street clothes, either arriving at or leaving a performance. The thinness of the figure is emphasized by the elongated format – created by the addition of a large extra piece of millboard at the bottom. The apparent immateriality of her figure is wittily set against the looming presence of a man's hat and coat seen hanging on the left.

The experimental combination of techniques employed here is comparable to

methods pioneered by Degas (see pp. 76–9). Lautrec laid in broad areas of the picture in oil paint, while the pastel elaboration allowed him to combine colour and drawing – simultaneously to sharpen the indication of the forms and to enrich the play of colour; this is most conspicuous around the figure's face and hat, where finer strokes of reds, yellows and greens are set off against the bold slashes of blue paint on the right in the background. These sharp colour relationships, together with the pallid yellow which lights the figure's face, heighten the sense of the artificiality typical of this world of urban entertainments.   J.H.

Courtauld Collection [P.1932.SC.465]

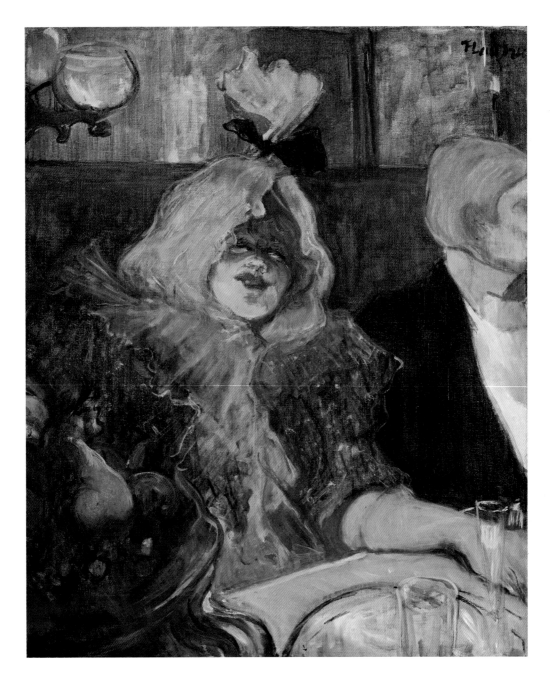

TOULOUSE-LAUTREC, HENRI DE
1864–1901
In the Private Booth 1899
Oil on canvas, 55.1 x 46
Signed, top right, initials in monogram:
'T-Lautrec'

The picture shows a *tête-à-tête* supper at the famous Rat Mort, a café and restaurant on the rue Pigalle in Paris, at the foot of the hill of Montmartre. By the late 1890s it retained a popular café downstairs, with a restaurant upstairs which was renowned for being a meeting place for stylish *demi-mondaines*. It is this that Lautrec portrayed here, his sitter being Lucy Jourdain, a celebrated *cocotte* of the day.

In the placing of the two figures, and particularly in the disconcerting device of cutting off the man's face with the picture frame, Lautrec has deliberately denied the viewer the possibility of reading a clear narrative into their relationship. Degas, in *L'Absinthe* (Musée d'Orsay, Paris), had earlier used a similar arrangement in order to suggest psychological distance and separation, but here the mood is less readily legible. The vivid red slash of the woman's smiling lips is echoed by the ebullient, flowing brushwork used to paint her garments and the bowl of fruit, creating a sense of vivacity as well as a rather startling analogy between woman and fruit. The effect is enhanced by the use of paint much

thinned with diluent and applied fluidly and transparently, exploiting the light tone of the ground. However, the seeming lack of focus in the woman's eyes, together with the man's averted gaze and the glass of champagne before her, may suggest that this gaiety is superficial. The artificiality of her position is emphasized by her fancy stage costume, in contrast to her companion's formal evening dress. These signs would have made it clear to contemporary viewers that this was a scene of *demi-mondaine* entertainment, but beyond that its mood and meaning are not closely fixed, leaving scope for individual interpretation. J.H.

Courtauld Collection [P.1948.SC.466]

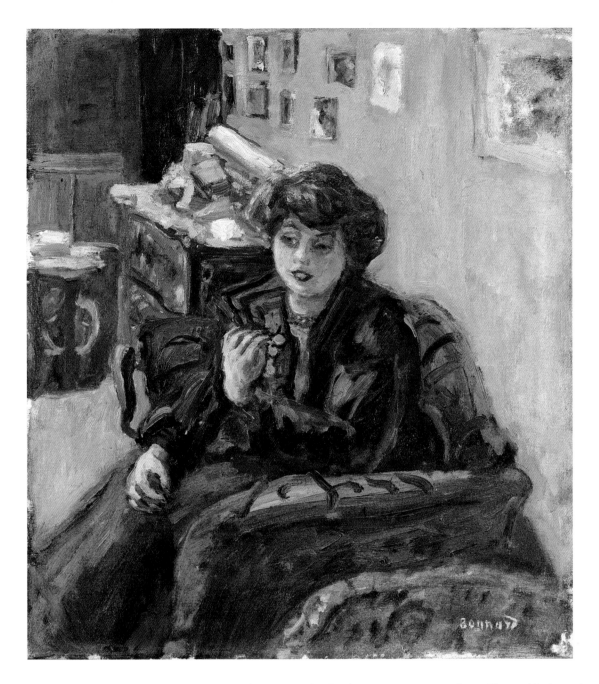

BONNARD, PIERRE 1867–1947
A Young Woman in an Interior 1906
Oil on canvas, 48.9 x 44.5
Signed, bottom right: 'Bonnard'

The sitter was the artist's mistress Marthe
Boursin, whom he married in 1925. After he
began to paint Marthe in 1894, she became
by far his most frequent model.

In its freely brushed surfaces, the picture
reveals Bonnard's return to a handling closer
to Impressionism, in contrast to the tighter
drawing and flatter paint surfaces of his

paintings of the 1890s. This development
marked a turn away from a Symbolist quest
to find the essential form for each subject, in
favour of a more straightforwardly
naturalistic approach.

Here, the subject is on the boundaries
between portraiture and genre painting.
The sitter is presented as a type, not as a
characterized individual, placed amid the
informal contents of a domestic interior –
perhaps the artist's studio. However, her pose
and expression do not tell any story or evoke
any particular mood. She holds something

up in front of her, and looks out beyond it,
but we cannot be sure what she holds
(a bunch of grapes or flowers?), or what she
is looking at. The angle of vision, close to
the model and looking down on her from
the side, increases the air of informality; the
lighting focuses more sharply on the
furniture in the background than on the
figure itself. By these calculated devices,
Bonnard created a seemingly casual image
of everyday domestic life.   J.H.

Fry Collection [P.1935.RF.32]

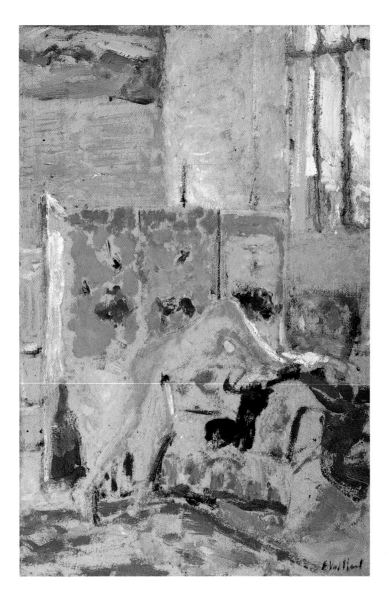

VUILLARD, EDOUARD 1868–1940
Interior: The Screen c.1909–10
Oil (*peinture à l'essence*) on paper, laid down on panel, 35.8 x 23.8
Signed, bottom right: 'E. Vuillard'

The subject of this picture is a nude model in an artist's studio. The figure is caught between poses, in an awkward gesture as she reaches across a sofa for her clothes. This theme, of an artist's model depicted off-guard, was very common in Salon painting in France during the 1880s, in works by artists such as Edouard Dantan. The appeal of such paintings was overtly voyeuristic. The viewer was offered a glimpse of the naked model at a moment when her nakedness was not legitimized and defused by assuming a formal artistic pose – by becoming a 'nude'.

However, Vuillard, in turn, has here undermined the conventional associations of the subject, by the way in which the figure is treated. The whole image is handled in a very summary way, and the figure is particularly lightly worked; paradoxically, the primary element in the composition is among the least defined. The woman's body is almost evoked in negative, which defuses the eroticism customarily associated with the theme. The richest colours appear in the screen, whose green, pink and blue panels set off the figure. By contrast, the form and location of the figure are suggested very summarily, by soft streaks of blue and by a few crisp highlights along her extended arm and her left thigh.

The window and the folding screen set up a grid-like structure extending across the whole picture, behind the curved shapes of

figure and sofa. The colour is quite muted, with true black used for the cushion or drapery on the sofa and elsewhere, in a tiny dab, to suggest the model's pubic hair. The surface of the painting is very matt, and happily has never been varnished, thus leaving it in the state which Vuillard would have wished.

Here Vuillard chose *peinture à l'essence* as his medium, in combination with an absorbent, fairly coarse, tinted paper, of which much of the surface was left exposed; and the essentially opaque pigment mixtures, such as those on the screen behind the figure, suggest the appearance of gouache. In those areas where the paint has not been so diluted, the surface retains the impasto of the brush-strokes.   J.H.

Courtauld Collection [P.1948.SC.481]

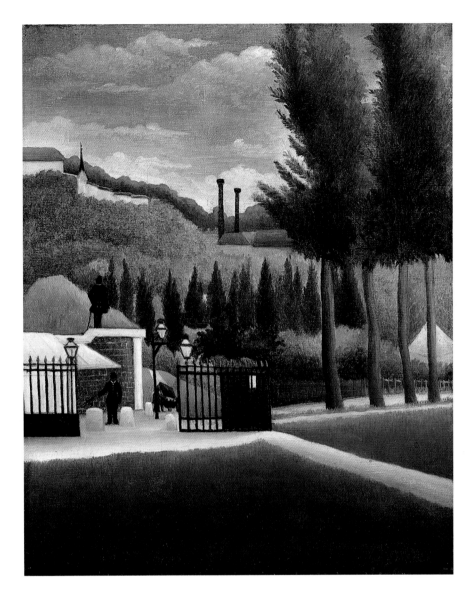

ROUSSEAU, HENRI ('Le Douanier')
1844–1910
The Toll-Gate c.1890?
Oil on canvas, 40.6 x 32.75
Signed, bottom right: 'H. Rousseau'

Rousseau served as a low-ranking customs official from 1871 to 1893, manning toll-gates (like the one seen here) on the outskirts of Paris. He began painting, untaught, c.1880; rejected by the Salon in 1885, he exhibited at the Société des Artistes Indépendants from 1886 and gradually became known in avant-garde circles. Only after the institution of the jury-free exhibition of the Indépendants could an artist like Rousseau hope to find an audience for his work.

His art has generally been viewed in the context of the avant-garde, but his initial models were the academic neo-classicists, Jean-Léon Gérôme and Charles Clément; apparently he sought their advice, and claimed that they had encouraged him to follow his own temperament. The precise definition of forms and smooth finish of his paintings correspond to the expectations of such masters. His few small outdoor studies belong to a long tradition of open-air sketching, and have no clear relationship to Impressionism, while his completed works are essentially academic in finish.

The subjects of his large pictures – exotic jungles (he never visited them in reality) and large-scale allegories – are also comparable to favoured themes in academic art. His many smaller landscapes such as *The Toll-Gate*, showing the everyday surroundings of the Parisian suburbs, often focus on distinctively modern elements, like the chimneys seen here, balloons, and (later) aeroplanes. These subjects are comparable to the suburban views painted by the Neo-Impressionists and other young independent artists in the 1880s and 1890s (see pp. 98–9).

Rousseau had little knowledge of conventional perspective; he suggests space by successions of planes stacked one on top of the other, so that objects on the horizon may still be defined as crisply as those nearby. Forms are treated as silhouettes, as in the case of the figures here, or as simple cylindrical tubes, like the tree-trunks. In this way, though, he was able to create paintings that are very tautly organized in two-dimensional terms: verticals and horizontals mesh into patterns of great coherence and real grandeur.

Such simplifications and stylizations would have seemed absurd to the academic masters of the nineteenth century, but they struck a chord with vanguard painters who rejected naturalistic depiction, first with Gauguin and his circle, then with Picasso and his friends. J.H.

Courtauld Collection [P.1948.SC.349]

MODIGLIANI, AMEDEO 1884–1920
Nude c.1916
Oil on canvas, 92.4 x 59.8
Signed, top left: 'Modigliani'

Modigliani's nudes combine poses that relate to the main traditions of Western art (to Manet, Ingres and others) with a type of drawing and execution which in its radical simplifications challenged the whole European figurative tradition. In *Nude*, the face is elongated, its features boldly simplified, in ways that reveal Modigliani's knowledge of Egyptian, African and Oceanic sculpture; yet the angle of the model's head recalls the very conventional imagery of the sleeping model, a favourite theme at the Salon exhibitions. Likewise the contours and modelling of the body are treated in simplified arabesques, but elements such as the breasts and the pubic hair are described more attentively.

Modigliani's brushwork is highly individual; characteristic scallop-shaped strokes are visible in the X-radiograph, the paint being applied with a short stabbing action. The paint has been manipulated while still wet, ploughed through with a stiff brush in the left background and around the outline of the head and, in the hair, scratched into with the end of the brush.

When a group of Modigliani's nudes were put on show at Berthe Weill's gallery in Paris in December 1917, the police first ordered the removal of the painting in the gallery window, and then the closure of the whole exhibition; apparently the prime cause of outrage was the artist's explicit rendering of pubic hair, a feature never present in the often very naturalistic depictions of the nude that were hung every year at the Salon without arousing any protests. This painting, with its combination of traditional and avant-garde elements, was one of the very few works in Samuel Courtauld's collection produced by a member of one of the avant-garde groups which emerged after 1900; Cubism and even Fauvism were outside the parameters of his taste.   J.H.

Courtauld Collection [P.1932.SC.271]

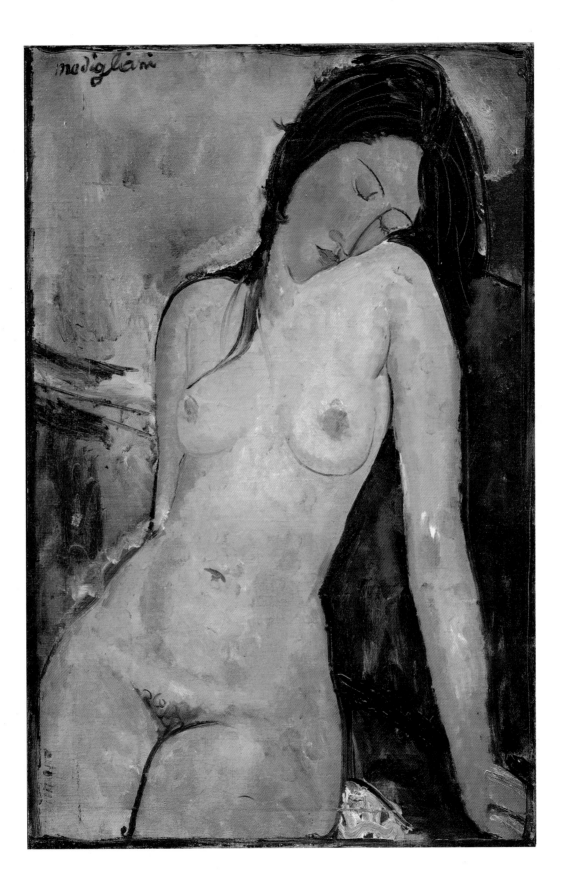

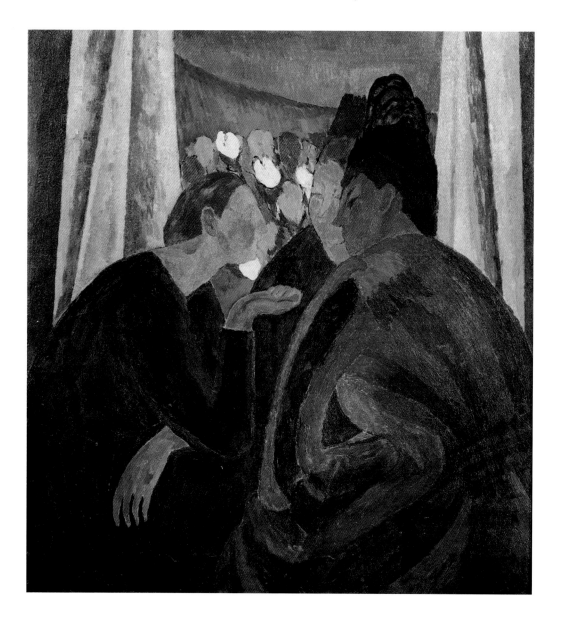

BELL, VANESSA 1879–1961
A Conversation 1913–16
Oil on canvas, 86.6 x 81

This painting has been known by three different titles: Roger Fry, who bought it from the artist, seems to have referred to it as *Visit*, whilst Virginia Woolf discusses it as *Three Women*; it is not clear where the title *A Conversation* originated, but the painting was known as this when it was bequeathed to the Courtauld Gallery in 1935.

The painting itself also has a history of change. Still visible beneath the paint surface of the figure to the left are the stripes that formerly decorated her blouse; likewise the swirling brush strokes in the curtain to the left suggest that this area may also originally have been patterned. In addition, technical analysis of the paint layers suggests that the figure to the right may originally have been a

man, seated in a chair, with a cane in his right hand. The fact that the work has clearly been extensively overpainted may explain the different dates that have been assigned to it. Vanessa Bell, much later, recalled having painted it in 1913, but the art historian Frances Spalding has suggested that it is more likely to have been painted towards, or even just after, the end of World War I. Since subsequent flaking of the paint surface suggests that the top layers may have been applied rather later, it may be that Bell altered the work some years after it was first painted.

The painting retains its original black, green, ochre and red frame, painted by Bell (this practice was popular among artists working in Fry's Omega Workshop, of which Bell was a co-director). The three women are shown engaged in earnest conversation, before a curtained window

through which a flower garden is visible. The curtains also add a theatrical air, lending the conversation an added sense of drama. Conversation was an art particularly cultivated by members of the Bloomsbury Group, who used it as a weapon against the moral attitudes of the previous generation. Having seen this painting, and others by Bell, in an exhibition, Virginia Woolf wrote to her sister:

> I had forgotten the extreme brilliancy and flow and wit and ardour of these works . . . I think you are a most remarkable painter. But I maintain that you are into the bargain, a satirist, a conveyer of impressions about human life: a short story writer of great wit and able to bring off a situation in a way that rouses my envy. I wonder if I could write the Three Women in prose?
>
> S.H.

Fry Collection [P.1935.RF.24]

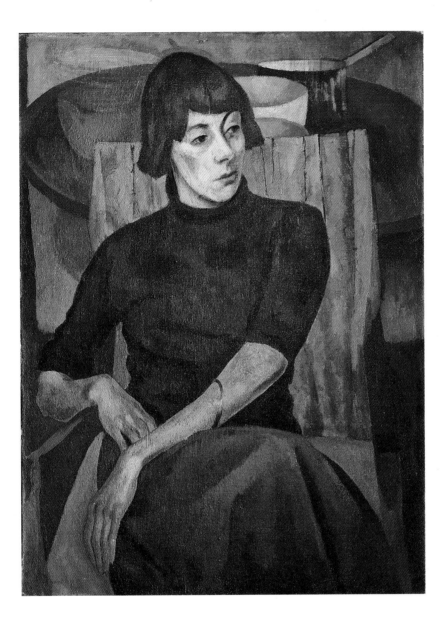

FRY, ROGER 1866–1934
Portrait of Nina Hamnett 1917
Oil on canvas, 82 x 61
Signed and dated

This painting is one of many contemporary representations of the artist Nina Hamnett who, through her flamboyant lifestyle, her 'rebel' persona and many love affairs, as well as her interest in avant-garde art, has acquired the label 'Queen of Bohemia'. Hamnett was working as an artist in London, and struggling with financial hardship when, in August 1913, she joined the Omega Workshops, which Roger Fry had founded earlier that year. One of Fry's aims had been to provide financial support for young artists by employing them to design and decorate items for domestic interiors, though he also wanted to apply the principles he derived from his study of

'Post-Impressionist' painting to interior design. However, apart from Vanessa Bell, most of the women at Omega were employed in a secondary capacity, to translate designs by male artists onto furniture, fabrics and lampshades, etc.

Hamnett also spent time in Paris, where she met and married Edgar de Bergen, known as Roald Kristian, as well as meeting many artists of the avant-garde, including Modigliani and Brancusi; the outbreak of war in 1914 forced her to return to London. In 1916 her friendship with Roger Fry developed into a brief love affair. Fry found in her someone who shared his intense interest in modern art, but one effect of the relationship was that Hamnett herself, like many women artists of the late nineteenth and early twentieth centuries, was, until recently, remembered mainly as the model and lover of a more celebrated male artist.

As travel became difficult during the war years, Fry turned his attention away from landscapes to portraiture and still lifes. Hamnett shared his interests, her own still-life painting moving towards abstraction; the shape of the saucepan in the background of this portrait also features prominently in one of her still lifes. Neither Hamnett nor Fry were chiefly concerned with producing likeness in portraiture; Fry aimed at 'imaginative characterization', whilst Hamnett wanted to paint 'psychological portraits that shall represent accurately the spirit of the age'. Hamnett is shown here as a modern woman, with 'bobbed' hair and unconventional clothes, serious minded, self-possessed and independent. Fry made several portraits of Hamnett, including drawings in the nude.   S.H.

Fry Collection [P.1935.RF.146]

123

KOKOSCHKA, OSKAR 1886–1980
Triptych: *The Myth of Prometheus* 1950
  Hades and Persephone (illustrated)
  The Apocalypse
  Prometheus
Mixed media on canvas, 238 x 233.8;
239 x 347.2; 239 x 233.6

The triptych, Kokoschka's largest work, was commissioned by Count Antoine Seilern as a ceiling painting for his London house, 56 Princes Gate, in Exhibition Road, and was painted on the premises. The project was first discussed in summer 1949, and by 20 September the artist had decided on a large central panel, to be followed 'in due course' by side panels. A few weeks before starting work, as Seilern later recalled, Kokoschka made a coloured chalk sketch, his very first idea for the painting, 'one evening. . . (if I remember rightly, on the floor), gave it to me and said: "that is how your ceiling is going to look".'

The centrepiece, *The Apocalypse*, was formally commissioned on 2 January 1950 for a fee of 17,500 Swiss francs, and

Kokoschka signed the contract on 14 January. By 8 February the work was completed and the artist asked whether he should paint the two wings straight away. Seilern agreed in a letter of 9 March to pay the same sum again, and suggested that before proceeding Kokoschka could study the completed canvas in its position on the ceiling; *The Apocalypse* was duly raised, and the wings were begun in mid-March. On 15 July the artist wrote: 'I put the last brush-stroke (I feel like saying axe-stroke) to my ceiling painting yesterday . . .'

The side pieces were apparently painted more or less simultaneously, probably starting with *Prometheus*. The theme of *Amor and Psyche* was originally intended to form the left wing, but was abandoned and completed five years later as an independent work; its substitute, *Hades and Persephone* (illustrated), was altered considerably at a very late stage and finished last.

The choice of subjects reflects the artist's growing fascination with ancient Greece as the source of humanism, an interest which was increasingly felt in his later work. He

wrote to J.P. Hodin: 'I wove like all three Fates in one person, in the cosmos I myself created. . . . The last of the three panels, with Demeter, Persephone and Hades, is the one I care about most, naturally, because it was the last, the one which completed my statement's great arc into the void, and rounds off the composition too, an organic whole in terms of both myth and form . . .'

In a last-minute alteration to this canvas, Kokoschka gave Hades his own likeness and added Medusa's head, an image of death, held in his hand. He entirely repainted Persephone, her face now a likeness of Konstanze, daughter of his friend Sebastian Isepp. She springs from the arms of Hades towards those of her mother Demeter who, with the arc of her body between Earth and the Underworld, expresses the regenerative forces of nature. This work is Kokoschka's most monumental statement concerning a lifelong fascination with mother-goddesses, symbolized by the moon above the enchanted landscape at the top.   H.B.

Princes Gate Collection [P.1978.PG.210]

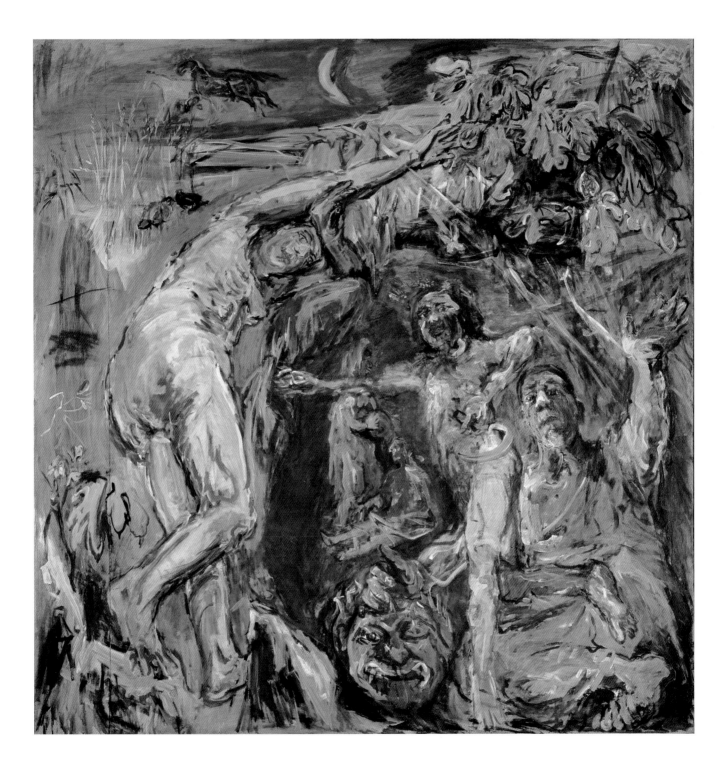

NICHOLSON, BEN 1894–1982
Painting 1937 1937
Oil on canvas, 79.5 x 91.5

Nicholson painted his first abstract pictures as early as 1924, but it was not until the mid-1930s that he refined his style to the extent of excluding all obvious figurative elements. He developed his abstract work in two closely related but distinct media: white-painted low reliefs, and easel pictures like *Painting 1937*.

Nicholson and the sculptors Henry Moore and Barbara Hepworth (Nicholson's second wife) were part of a small but influential community of artists living off Haverstock Hill in Hampstead; its members included such notable refugees as Naum Gabo, who came in 1935, and Piet Mondrian, who arrived in 1938. Nicholson had first visited Mondrian's studio in Paris in 1934, and had been greatly impressed not only by his work, but also by that of Picasso, Braque, Arp and Brancusi, all of whom he had met in the

course of several visits he made to Paris in the early 1930s.

Nicholson created his first white relief in 1934, and by 1935 his paintings had also become uncompromisingly geometrical. Of his reliefs he wrote: 'a square and a circle are nothing in themselves and are alive only in the instinctive and inspirational use an artist can make of them in expressing a poetic idea . . . You can create a most exciting tension between these forces . . .' (that is to say, the interplay of geometrical forms). This 'most exciting tension' also enlivens Nicholson's abstract paintings, indeed, one can say all his best work, but it is particularly relevant to *Painting 1937*, in which he carefully balances a strong red square and a black rectangle, offsetting them by a blue linking zone and the surrounding rectangles of softer colours. The overall effect is quite warm and markedly different from that of a larger, related work, also called *Painting 1937* (Tate Gallery, London), where, despite the use of a black, blue, yellow and red sequence of

rectangles on the right-hand side of the picture, a sense of coolness prevails.

The genesis of the Courtauld picture and of similar works may be seen in a series of highly geometricized still life on table-top compositions, and in yet another *Painting 1937* (Scottish National Gallery of Modern Art, Edinburgh), where vestiges of the table-legs are still shown. In some still lifes of 1934, the objects on the table, such as jugs, cups and plates, appear as highly stylized silhouette-like shapes, with some suggestion of textural variation on the painted surface.

Lady (Leslie) Martin, who once owned this painting, has recalled that the central square of yellow ochre/orange used to be a bright acid-yellow, presumably similar in colour to the yellow rectangle in the Tate painting. The artist must have used some additive to his pigment which has resulted in this unintended change occurring over a period of 60 years.   D.F.

Alistair Hunter Collection [P.1982.XX.286]

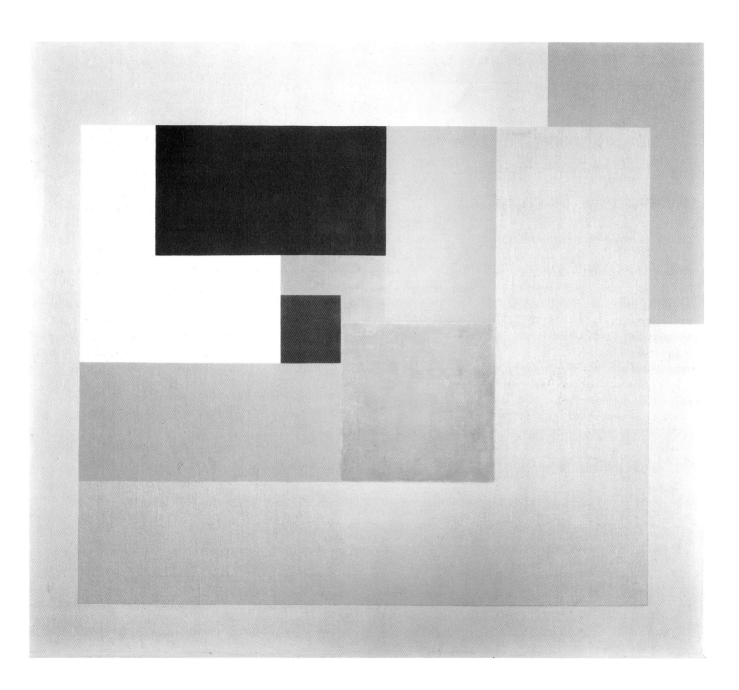

Index of Artists